OPTIMA

POSITIVE HEALTH GUIDE

THE
HIGH-FIBRE
COOKBOOK
RECIPES FOR GOOD HEALTH
Pamela Westland

Introduction by Dr Denis Burkitt

Foreword by Nathan Pritikin
Director of the Pritikin Longevity Center, California

© Pamela Westland 1982

First published in 1982 by
Martin Dunitz Limited
Reprinted 1982 (three times), 1983 (three times), 1984, 1985 (twice)

This edition published in 1988 by
Macdonald Optima, a division of
Macdonald & Co. (Publishers) Ltd

Reprinted 1990

A member of Maxwell Macmillan Pergamon Publishing Corporation

British Library Cataloguing in Publication Data

Westland, Pamela
    The high-fibre cookbook: recipes for good
    health. —(Positive health guide)
    1. High-fibre diet – Recipes
    I. Title   II. Series
    641.5′637   RM237.6

    ISBN 0-356-14490-9

Macdonald & Co. (Publishers) Ltd
Orbit House
1 New Fetter Lane
London EC4A 1AR

Photoset in Plantin

Printed and bound in Singapore.

Chief dietetic consultant: Dr Pat Judd, Department of Nutrition,
Queen Elizabeth College, London University

Design and line drawings by Rose and Lamb Design Partnership

Photographs by Bob Komar; styling by Wendy Morris; food preparation by
Hilary Walden

*Front cover photograph shows Chicken and bean paella (centre, see p. 94), and
Stuffed aubergines (below, see p. 68)*

CONTENTS

FOREWORD

Nathan Pritikin, Director, Pritikin Longevity Centre, California

At last! A cookbook for the high-fibre way of eating, inspired by Dr Denis Burkitt, the man who almost single-handedly started to educate the developed nations away from processed foods.

Constipation is one of the commonest ailments in developed Western countries. Our food is highly processed to remove the roughage, or dietary fibre, that is present in all grains. In the milling of wheat, rice, and corn, not only the dietary fibre is removed that is so essential for normal bowel function, but also much of the vitamin and mineral content is lost.

Lack of adequate fibre has been implicated in many types of colon disease; and in countries where fibre is not removed from the foods, these colon problems – as Denis Burkitt explains in his introduction – are practically non-existent. Colon cancer has been rising steadily in the developed nations, and hopefully a return to natural unprocessed grains will reverse that trend.

I knew Denis Burkitt through his writings years before I met him. When I read his article in *The Lancet* on 'Relationship as a Clue to Causation' (December 12, 1970), I was fascinated by his brilliant logic. He had built a step-by-step case relying on observation and reason, and in one bold move, had swept away the confusion surrounding the origins and prevention of degenerative diseases.

In the last ten years, health professionals in the developed nations have been convinced by Dr Burkitt's writings and are now in ever increasing numbers advocating a return to the past, to the unrefined high-fibre foods; especially to cereals such as whole groat oats, wheat and bran, brown rice, barley, millet, and corn.

My team in Santa Barbara, California, was pleased to find that a number of types of recipes in the book were completely new to them. Moreover, the directions were easy to follow, and I and my staff are convinced that whole-grain food preparation will grow in popularity and win hearts and appetites around the world.

INTRODUCTION

Denis Burkitt, MD, BSc (Hon), FRCS, FRCPI (Hon), FRS

This is no ordinary cookbook. Its aim is to help you to stay healthy by changing the emphasis of your day-to-day diet away from refined foods towards those which have a high dietary fibre and a relatively low fat and sugar content.

By way of introduction I would like to explain why I consider this change so essential, and to show why fibre is so important in maintaining good health.

Through observations made in many countries over a long period, I have become increasingly convinced that changes in the basic composition of diets in Western countries could be of incalculable value in improving general health in these communities. It has only recently become generally accepted that a formidable list of the commonest diseases in more affluent societies are rare in rural communities in the Third World, and yet are comparably prevalent among both black and white Americans. Moreover, these same diseases were uncommon even in Western countries before the first quarter of this century. Extensive studies of disease distribution throughout the world have clearly and consistently demonstrated that these diseases are directly related to some aspect of modern Western life.

The term 'Western diseases' includes ailments of such major importance as coronary heart disease, the commonest cause of death; large bowel cancer, which together with lung cancer (which results largely from cigarette smoking) are the commonest causes of death from cancer; appendicitis and diverticular disease of the colon, which are the commonest disorders of the intestine; gall-stones, the commonest reason for abdominal surgery; diabetes, the commonest metabolic disorder; obesity, the commonest nutritional disorder; haemorrhoids and varicose veins, which are among the most prevalent Western complaints; and tooth decay, the commonest of all diseases.

The geography and history of these diseases shows that to a large extent they must be preventable once the factors which cause them are identified and reduced or eliminated. There are of course an enormous variety of changes that are associated with increased affluence and all the benefits of modern technology. But since all the disorders mentioned above have been shown to be related to changes that take place in the body's digestive system, it would seem logical to consider dietary changes that have been shown to precede the emergence or increased prevalence of these diseases before investigating other environmental factors.

In Western countries, greater changes have been made in the basic composition of diet over the last 200 years than during the whole of man's previous existence on earth. To put it simply, we have filled our stomachs with foods to which our constitution is not adapted and our modern diseases may well be some of the inevitable results. Adaptation is a slow process, and there is no point in hopefully waiting to adapt. We must recognise the faulty steps we have taken and retrace them sufficiently far to reduce the factors responsible for these diseases.

The following are the major contrasts between diets of the Third World, where these diseases are least prevalent, and the West, where they are most common.

Protein While the amount consumed is roughly comparable in both societies, its source in the West is largely animal; in the Third World, mostly vegetable. We in the West are eating more meat, eggs and cheese at the expense of beans and vegetables.

Carbohydrate Western intake is substantially lower, most coming from sugar (in the form of table sugar and sugar in cakes, etc) rather than starch, which comes from grain cereals, root vegetables and beans.

Fat Intake, mostly in the form of butter, margarine, oils, and fat in meat, is currently three times greater in affluent than in poorer communities.

Fibre This is the most important difference of all, consumption in Western countries being only a third to a sixth of that in the Third World.

Dietary fibre is the substance which forms the cell wall and rigid structure of all plant foods. It was little understood until a little over a decade ago, and because it was non-nutritious and its enormously important properties had not been recognised it was deliberately removed from our food to give the food what was considered a more pleasing texture and appearance. The main casualty was wheat, from which the fibre-rich bran was milled away to make white bread.

Fibre exerts its beneficial effect on the digestive system in part by increasing the volume and softness of bowel content and hastening its passage through the gut, thus preventing constipation; a deficiency in cereal fibre in particular is the major cause of this complaint. In addition, fibre influences greatly the bowel's bacterial content and has profound effects on the metabolism and absorption of substances in the bowel. There is strong evidence that by these and other actions dietary fibre affords some protection against all the diseases listed above. Excessive fat in the diet has also been incriminated in the causation of some, as has excessive sugar. It is important to remember that a fibre-rich diet is almost invariably low in fat and vice versa.

We thus have definite pointers as to how we may retrace some of the disastrous dietetic steps that have been taken over the last two centuries in Western countries, but we must not place exclusive emphasis on any single aspect. When improving our diet we should make the following changes. Most important in my opinion, increase fibre intake, putting maximum emphasis on cereal fibre, as this has the greatest effect in combatting constipation; simultaneously reduce consumption of fat and sugar; and finally, it would be wise to cut down on salt, in view of the growing evidence relating it to high blood pressure. A general guide – in line with current Western nutritional thinking – would be for Western communities to double their starch and fibre intake, halve their sugar and salt, and reduce their fat by a third (a greater fat reduction, though beneficial, would not be palatably acceptable). There is a more detailed guide, linked to the nutritional analyses of the book's recipes, on the next page.

Being an advocate of the value of high-fibre diets, I am often asked how to go about getting more fibre into everyday meals. Unfortunately, beyond recommending eating more wholemeal bread, fibre-rich breakfast cereals, beans, root vegetables and brown rice, I do not have the credentials to offer more specific advice on cookery. This book, however, has the answer. It offers a great variety of high-fibre recipes which not only provide a practical way of attaining the dietary goals I have described, but will also prove, I am sure, that high-fibre cooking can be economical, versatile and, above all, delicious.

PLANNING A HIGH-FIBRE DIET

Dr Pat Judd, Department of Nutrition, Queen Elizabeth College, London University

The recipes in this book have been designed to help you increase the fibre content of your diet, not just by adding back the bran removed on milling cereals, but by eating a wide variety of foods which are naturally high in dietary fibre. As far as possible, current nutritional thinking in other areas has also been followed: most of the recipes use less meat, fat and sugar than comparable recipes in other cookery books. Accompanying each recipe are the calorie, fat and fibre values per portion; these figures are not absolutely precise, but they give a rough idea of the value of each recipe in terms of these important constituents.

If you want to move towards Dr Burkitt's suggestions for a healthier diet, made in the introduction, here are a few points to watch:

1) Dietary fibre The average Western intake of dietary fibre is around 20 g a day. Many authorities believe that 30–35 g would be a better level to aim for. Remember that as well as the fibre obtained from the dishes made from the recipes in this book, you will also be getting some from the rest of your diet. A 50-g/2-oz slice of bread provides about 4 g if it's wholemeal (only 1 g if it's white). Other grain-based foods – as well as beans, vegetables and fruit – eaten with the meals will also increase your fibre intake. 20 g/⅔ oz All-Bran, for example, contains around 5 g fibre; 50 g/2 oz kidney beans provides 4 g; 75 g/3 oz fresh spinach gives 6 g; and 25 g/1 oz dried prunes have 5 g fibre. For more information on fibre values and the benefits of high-fibre eating, see a companion volume by Dr Burkitt called *Don't Forget Fibre in Your Diet.*

2) Fat Most people eat more fat than they really need. Currently, it is suggested that we should only get about a third of our calories from fat. For a moderately active person this amounts to less than 100 g fat each day for a woman; around 120 g a day for a man. You can therefore use the values given with the recipes to see if you are overdoing the fat. Remember that you also obtain fat from other foods you eat – 290 ml/½ pint of ordinary milk will supply about 10 g of fat, a teaspoon of butter or margarine about 5 g. Some of the recipes – the cakes, pies and pastries, in particular – are relatively high in fat, and hence calories, and should really be saved for special occasions.

3) Calories People's energy requirements vary enormously. One person's slimming diet may be one on which his neighbour would gain weight. If you are trying to lose weight or just to maintain it but know you put on pounds easily, then stick to the recipes with the lowest calorie values.

Most reducing diets allow somewhere between 1,000 and 1,500 calories per day. By this reckoning your three main meals should supply 300–400 calories each to allow some leeway for milk in drinks and perhaps a snack of fruit in between. If one of the recipes is high in calories then match it with lower ones at the next meal. A high-fibre diet will help you keep to your reducing programme; the meals tend to be filling and you should find it is longer before you become hungry again. Some of the portions in the recipes are generous and you may find that you will be satisfied with a smaller amount, thus reducing your calorie intake even further.

1 HIGH-FIBRE COOKING

How can the high-fibre way of eating fit into *your* busy family life? The answer is, easily. It does not necessarily mean making radical changes in the foods you have enjoyed. You don't have to give up eating meat entirely, nor even puddings. You can continue to enjoy all these things, though in moderation.

What you do have to do is change the emphasis, get used to eating more of some foods that are high in fibre, and less of others that are high in sugar and fats.

First of all, switch to wholemeal flour for all your baking. A very simple step, but an important one, because wholemeal flour has not had all the valuable dietary fibre sifted out of it.

Make your own bread if you possibly can. If time is short, make soda bread that doesn't need pre-baking time to rise. Eat more bread with less fat on it. Switch from butter or margarine to low-fat spread, and use just a light scraping. Home-made wholemeal bread is so delicious, you won't notice the lack of fat.

Get into the habit of making all your pastry with wholemeal flour. There are several different recipes in the following chapters. Try them all and then adopt your favourite, the one that comes most easily, as your basic. Then mix and match the different fillings, and use the pastry with your own family's favourite fillings. You will find wholemeal pastry a new experience. It is slightly heavier than pastry made with bleached and refined flour and does not rise so much. But it has a delicious nutty flavour that goes well with both sweet and savoury ingredients. When making wholemeal pastry a good way of overcoming the problem of making holes in the dough when rolling it out is to roll it between sheets of polythene or greaseproof paper.

Serve breakfast cereals with low-fat plain yoghurt or unsweetened fruit juice as a change from milk, and with dried or fresh fruits, muesli-style. All-Bran cereal can also be used to thicken savoury dishes, as a topping on baked vegetable and pasta dishes, to flavour fruit and yoghurt drinks, and in bread, cakes and pastry. (You can add up to 50 g/2 oz All-Bran to each 450 g/1 lb wholemeal flour.)

Change to wholemeal pasta – you can buy it in spaghetti, macaroni and fancy shapes – and brown rice. They both take a little longer to cook than their refined counterparts, but are higher in dietary fibre and more filling, so you actually eat less, yet feel more satisfied.

Don't be worried about serving pasta and rice – they are not themselves high in calories. The danger comes in the things you serve with them. Vegetable and chicken sauces, for example, are lower in fat than red meat and creamy ones, and especially good with wholemeal pasta and brown rice.

Use wholemeal flour, wholemeal semolina or bran to thicken sauces, gravy and stews, and even fruit purée and juices. Again, it gives a slightly nutty flavour which you will soon come to appreciate.

Serve vegetables and fruit with the skins intact whenever possible. This means just scrubbing potatoes – unless they are to be mashed, when they do need peeling – carrots and parsnips. Less work, more fibre. And even in fruit salad, leave the skins on fruits like apples, pears and peaches.

Plan your meals so that you serve a dish using pulses about three times a week. There is an enormous variety of dried peas, beans and lentils, from the bright red little aduki beans to the round nut-sized chick peas. You can use them all in soups, casseroles, curries and salads, and they are all high in both fibre and protein.

You can cut down on the amount of meat you serve without even noticing it if you add bulk to the dishes with pulses, vegetables, wholemeal pasta and brown rice. Meat is not only expensive – it is deceptively high in fat. Even lean meat has hidden fat.

Use a good non-stick frying-pan and dry-fry minced or cubed meat to draw off the fat. Then discard it before adding vegetables or other ingredients.

A good quality non-stick frying-pan is, indeed, the best kitchen investment you can make. That way, you can dry-fry vegetables for soups and casseroles; sweat onions, mushrooms and tomatoes; and really cut down on calories. And you can make wholemeal pancakes and pizzas, potato cakes and all kinds of hot snacks with no added fat. If your pan is not absolutely efficient when used dry, wipe it with the slightest smear of fat first.

The quantity of salt you use is a matter of taste, but a matter of health too. Keep it to an absolute minimum in your cooking and try to discourage the family from adding more at the table.

Keep a wary eye on all dairy products, and choose those with the lowest fat content. Substituting skimmed milk for ordinary pasteurized milk makes a wealth of difference in calorie and fat terms.

Choosing low-fat plain yoghurt, or making your own with milk powder and water (skimmed milk is not at all satisfactory), gives you a very versatile ingredient. Use yoghurt with unsweetened fruit juices for salad dressings that are much healthier and lighter than oil-rich ones. Use it in place of cream in soups, sauces and puddings. And serve it, with fruit purée, as a delightful dessert in its own right.

Make your own wholemeal cakes and you can control the fibre, fat and sugar content. Using dried fruits in cakes and puddings gives you sweetness plus fibre, the formula to look for.

Keep high-calorie cakes and puddings for rare occasions, and have plainer, blander ones for every day. That's what is meant by a switch of emphasis. And things you have only rarely become more of a pleasure, more of a luxury.

In general, you will find that a high-fibre diet is no hardship at all – unlike so many other diets. Quite the reverse, in fact, because all the ingredients are so naturally delicious.

Just one word of warning. Do not fall into the trap of thinking that if you add fibre in the form of bran to a dish, then the rest of the ingredients will be fine. No so! You do need fibre, but you do not need added fats and sugars. Let your energy and vitality come naturally from the good, low-fat ingredients. As the following recipes show, there are plenty to choose from.

2 GOOD MORNING BREAKFAST

Breakfast is probably the most neglected meal of the day. In the rush to arrive punctually at work or school many people find they only have time to grab a quick cup of coffee or tea on their way out.

You only need to get up a little earlier to have a breakfast that will supply your body with sufficient nutrients for you to function efficiently throughout the morning.

A good filling breakfast will also help you to avoid eating unnecessary snacks before lunch; and school children will be less tempted during the morning by sweets and chocolate bars.

Breakfast cereals are an excellent way to start the day, especially if you have little time. The are quick and easy to prepare, provide essential vitamins, and when mixed with bran and fresh or dried fruit they become an appetizing high-fibre dish. They are so simple to make that I have included just a few recipes to give you a starting point to develop your own ideas.

Serve low-fat plain yoghurt or soft cheese or unsweetened fruit juices with cereals and fruit salads.

Make your own low-fat yoghurt from milk powder (see page 14) and flavour it with fresh or dried fruits or fruit purée.

Prepare fruit salads overnight to save precious morning moments. If they are chilled, they will be more refreshing.

Liquidize fruit with yoghurt and added bran – another overnight idea – to provide a breakfast for people who either do not have much time in the morning, or who can't face solid food to start the day.

Fruit provides more fibre than fruit juice.

Half a grapefruit and some wholemeal toast is a simple, ordinary breakfast that has a good fibre content.

As a change from toast, make a weekly supply of whole-grain biscuits or crispbreads – lovely with slices of fresh fruit.

Roll out a batch of wholemeal scones ready to bake for 10 minutes in the morning for a hot breakfast with a difference.

With toast, biscuits or scones, serve low-fat spread or soft cheese and a pot of thick fruit purée.

If you do, occasionally, have a traditional cooked breakfast choose items which are grilled rather than fried and have mushrooms and tomatoes in preference to fat-rich foods.

If you do fry anything, use a non-stick pan so there will not be any need for extra fat.

FRUITY BRAN

SERVES 4
Per serving: 170 Cals, 5 g fat, 11 g fibre

100 g/4 oz All-Bran
30 ml/2 tbsp rolled oats
25 g/1 oz seedless raisins
50 g/2 oz dried apricots, chopped
25 g/1 oz walnuts, roughly chopped

To serve:
unsweetened apple juice

Mix all the ingredients together and serve with chilled apple juice. Skimmed milk, low-fat plain yoghurt or other unsweetened fruit juices can be served instead.

You can store the bran and fruit mixture in a screw-topped jar.

FRUIT FLAKES

SERVES 4
Per serving: 140 Cals, 2 g fat, 9 g fibre

75 g/3 oz Bran Flakes
25 g/1 oz All-Bran
25 g/1 oz rolled oats
50 g/2 oz stoned dates, chopped
2 apples, cored and grated

To serve:
low-fat plain yoghurt

Mix together the cereals and dates. This can be done in advance and the mixture stored in a screw-topped jar. To serve, stir in the grated apple and mix with chilled yoghurt.

Alternative suggestion
Serve with unsweetened fruit juices or skimmed milk.

See photograph on pp.16–17.

FRESH FRUIT BOWL

SERVES 6
Per serving: 145 Cals, 5 g fat, 4 g fibre

50 g/2 oz seedless white grapes
1 orange, segmented
2 dessert apples, grated
2 bananas, sliced
15 ml/1 tbsp lemon juice
15 g/½ oz cashew nuts
25 g/1 oz hazelnuts
40 g/1½ oz raisins
100 g/4 oz Bran Flakes
30 ml/2 tbsp wheat germ
275 ml/10 fl oz low-fat plain
  yoghurt

To serve:
unsweetened grape juice

Mix together the grapes and orange. Stir the grated apple and bananas into the lemon juice. Toss them with the fruit and nuts and then with the Bran Flakes and wheat germ.

Just before serving, stir the yoghurt into the cereal and fruit mixture and serve with grape juice or other unsweetened fruit juice.

FRUIT AND NUT BRAN

SERVES 6
Per serving: 245 Cals, 8 g fat, 10 g fibre

75 g/3 oz All-Bran
25 g/1 oz rolled oats
25 g/1 oz seedless raisins
15 g/½ oz sultanas
25 g/1 oz dried apricots,
  chopped
15 g/½ oz dried apple flakes
25 g/1 oz stoned dates, chopped
25 g/1 oz walnuts, roughly
  chopped
15 g/½ oz cashew nuts

To serve:
low-fat plain yoghurt

Garnish:
30 ml/2 tbsp desiccated
  coconut, optional

Mix together the cereals, fruit and nuts. Just before serving, stir in the yoghurt, or serve it separately so that the cereal is at its crunchiest. Toasted coconut makes a pleasant contrast of texture and flavour.

PORRIDGE

SERVES 4
Per serving: 100 Cals, 2 g fat,
2 g fibre

1 litre/1¾ pints water
100 g/4 oz rolled oats
10 ml/2 tsp salt

Measure the water into a pan, sprinkle on the oats and salt and bring to the boil, stirring. Simmer for 4 minutes, stirring occasionally.

OATMEAL PORRIDGE

SERVES 4
Per serving: 100 Cals, 2 g fat,
2 g fibre

1 litre/1¾ pints boiling water
10 ml/2 tsp salt
100 g/4 oz fine, medium or
coarse oatmeal

Pour the boiling water into a pan, add the salt then gradually stir in the oatmeal. Stir over moderate heat until the mixture starts to thicken. Lower the heat and simmer for 20 minutes, stirring occasionally.

YOGHURT

MAKES 1 litre/1¾ pints
Per 275 ml/½ pint: 170 Cals,
10 g fat, 0 g fibre

1 litre/1¾ pints milk (or, for
low-fat yoghurt, milk
powder and water mixed
according to instructions
on the tin)
30 ml/2 tbsp low-fat plain
yoghurt, from a previous
batch, or commercially
made

Bring the milk or milk powder and water mixture to the boil and leave to cool to 43°C/110°F. At this point you will be able to dip in your finger without its feeling hot. Stir in the yoghurt 'starter' and pour into a wide-necked vacuum flask or a bowl. Cover the flask or bowl and leave undisturbed (the bowl in a warm place) for 8–10 hours. Store the yoghurt in the refrigerator for up to 7 days, reserving a little for the next batch.

Use yoghurt as a substitute for cream, in baking, as a topping, a garnish, to make drinks (see pages 19–21) and as a dish in its own right.

CITRUS CUPS

SERVES 4
Per serving: 130 Cals, 3 g fat,
6 g fibre

8 prunes
120 ml/8 tbsp unsweetened
orange juice
2 pink grapefruit, segmented
2 oranges, segmented

Garnish:
25 g/1 oz walnuts, chopped

Soak the prunes for at least 1 hour in the orange juice. Strain, reserving any juices and cut in half. Discard the stones.

Mix the prunes with the grapefruit, oranges and any remaining orange juice and chill.

Spoon into halved grapefruit shells or a serving dish. Top with chopped nuts.

See photograph on pp.16–17.

MUESLI BASE

SERVES 4
Per serving: 120 Cals, 2 g fat, 4 g fibre

75 g/3 oz rolled oats
15 g/½ oz bran
15 g/½ oz wheat germ
25 g/1 oz Bran Flakes

Mix these dry ingredients together to make 4 generous servings, or experiment with other combinations of grains.

Serving suggestions
The base can be varied daily by simply adding grated apple, a selection of fresh or dried fruits, nuts or vegetables, and serving it with cold milk, unsweetened lemon, orange, apple or grape juice, or low-fat plain yoghurt.

FRESH FRUIT MUESLI

SERVES 6
Per serving: 150 Cals, 4 g fat, 6 g fibre

150 ml/5 fl oz hot water
juice 1 lemon
50 g/2 oz seedless raisins
2 apples
2 bananas
1 orange
50 g/2 oz grapes
1 recipe muesli base (see above)
25 g/1 oz mixed nuts

To serve:
unsweetened orange, apple or grape juice

Pour the water and lemon juice over the raisins and leave to soak while preparing the fruit. Core and slice the apples, slice the bananas, divide the orange into segments and seed the grapes. Mix with the raisins.
Put the muesli base into a bowl, pour on the fruit, add the nuts and mix well. Serve with the fruit juice.

TOASTED MUESLI

SERVES 6
Per serving: 160 Cals, 8 g fat, 3 g fibre

1 recipe muesli base (see above)
15 ml/1 tbsp clear honey
15 ml/1 tbsp brown sugar
10 ml/2 tsp vegetable oil, e.g. sunflower
few drops vanilla essence
50 g/2 oz mixed nuts, chopped

To serve:
fresh or dried fruit and more nuts

Heat the oven to 180°C/350°F/Gas 4. Put the honey and sugar into a small pan over low heat and stir until they dissolve. Remove the pan from the heat, add the oil, vanilla essence and nuts and stir in the muesli base.
Spread the muesli on a baking tray and bake for about 20 minutes, stirring occasionally so that it browns evenly. Allow to cool on the tray. Serve with fresh or dried fruits and more nuts. This muesli can be stored in a covered jar.

OVERLEAF: Fruit flakes (*left*, see p. 12), **Fresh fruit muesli** (*centre*) **Citrus cups** (*right*, see p.14).

GRAPEFRUIT MARMALADE

MAKES APPROX 4.5 kg/10 lb
Per oz: 10 Cals, negligible fat
and fibre

1.25 kg/2¾ lb grapefruit
2 lemons
5 ml/1 tsp tartaric or citric
acid
3.1 litres/5½ pints water
2.75 kg/6 lb brown sugar

Wash or scrub the grapefruits and lemons, cut in half and squeeze the juice. Scrape off the fruit pulp, cut the peel into thick slices and tie the pips in a piece of scalded muslin or cheesecloth. Put everything in a pan with the acid and water and then bring to the boil and simmer for about 2 hours, or until the peel is tender and the contents of the pan reduced by half. Remove the bag of pips and squeeze to extract all the liquid.

Add the sugar and stir over low heat until dissolved. Bring to the boil and then, stirring frequently, boil until the marmalade is dark brown and thick.

To test if it is ready, put a little on a saucer and leave it to cool, then push a finger across the surface to see if 'ripples' appear. Leave it in the pan to cool for about 15 minutes, then stir well to distribute the grapefruit and lemon peel.

Pour into warm jars, cover with waxed discs and transparent paper covers or screw-on lids. Label with the contents and date. Store in a cool, dry place.

This marmalade has a high sugar content, so use it sparingly, as with all other preserves that have those hidden but tempting calories.

Oranges or a mixture of other citrus fruits could equally well be used.

GRAPEFRUIT AND APRICOT SALAD

SERVES 4
Per serving: 90 Cals, 0 g fat,
8 g fibre

100 g/4 oz dried apricots,
soaked and drained
2 grapefruit, segmented
2 apples, cored and thinly
sliced
juice 1 orange

Toss the apricots with the grapefruit, sliced apple and orange juice. Cover and chill.

BREAKFAST SALAD

SERVES 4
Per serving: 190 Cals, 1 g fat,
5 g fibre

2 grapefruit, segmented
2 oranges, segmented
2 bananas, sliced
6-8 dates, chopped
425 ml/15 fl oz low-fat plain
yoghurt

Stir the fruit into the yoghurt, cover and chill. Serve, if liked, with a pinch of cinnamon.

Serving suggestion
Crunchy biscuits, such as rich oatmeal biscuits (page 22), are a good accompaniment.

Garnish:
pinch cinnamon (optional)

18

MORNING MALTER

SERVES 4
Per serving: 185 Cals, 4 g fat,
5 g fibre

60 ml/4 tbsp malted milk
  powder
575 ml/1 pint low-fat plain
  yoghurt, chilled
30 ml/2 tbsp bran
2.5 ml/½ tsp grated nutmeg
25 g/1 oz walnuts, chopped

Garnish:
1 banana
15 ml/1 tbsp rolled oats

Put the milk powder, yoghurt, bran and nutmeg into a blender and mix until well blended. Stir in the chopped walnuts and divide between 4 glasses or mugs. Decorate with slices of banana and rolled oats.

SPICED APPLE YOGHURT

SERVES 4
Per serving: 130 Cals, 2 g fat,
4 g fibre

4 apples
575 ml/1 pint low-fat plain
  yoghurt, chilled
2.5 ml/½ tsp ground cinnamon
pinch grated nutmeg
15 ml/1 tbsp bran

Core the apples. Slice 3 and put them into a blender with the other ingredients. Mix until smooth. Chop the remaining apple and stir into the drink. Pour into individual mugs or glasses and sprinkle with a pinch of nutmeg.

ORANGE WHIZZ

SERVES 4
Per serving: 140 Cals, 3 g fat,
4 g fibre

4 oranges
575 ml/1 pint low-fat plain
  yoghurt, chilled
1 egg
15 ml/1 tbsp bran

Grate 10 ml/2 tsp of the orange rind then peel and segment the oranges. Put the segments into a blender with the other ingredients and mix until smooth. Pour into individual mugs or glasses and sprinkle with the orange rind.

DRIED FRUIT FOAM

SERVES 4
Per serving: 60 Cals, 2 g fat,
6 g fibre

100 g/4 oz cooked dried fruits
such as apricots, peaches
and pears
575 ml/1 pint low-fat plain
yoghurt, chilled
pinch ground cloves
1 egg
15 ml/1 tbsp bran
25 g/1 oz dried apricots, finely
chopped

Put all the ingredients except the chopped apricots into a blender and blend until smooth. Stir in the chopped apricots and pour into individual mugs or glasses. Sprinkle with a small pinch of ground cloves.

BLACKBERRY SHAKE

SERVES 4
Per serving: 60 Cals, 1 g fat,
7 g fibre

275 ml/½ pint blackberry
purée (or raspberry,
strawberry or blackcurrant
purée)
275 ml/10 fl oz low-fat plain
yoghurt, chilled
juice 1 lemon
15 ml/1 tbsp bran

Decoration:
a few blackberries or other
soft fruit if available

Put all the ingredients except the blackberries into a blender and blend until well mixed. Pour the drink into individual glasses or mugs and decorate with the berries.

BANANA BRAN

SERVES 4
Per serving: 140 Cals, 3 g fat,
3 g fibre

575 ml/1 pint low-fat plain
yoghurt, chilled
2 large bananas
1 egg
15 ml/1 tbsp bran and extra
for topping

Put all the ingredients into a blender and mix until smooth. Pour into individual mugs or glasses and sprinkle with a little extra bran.

Blackberry shake (*bottom*),
Dried fruit foam (*top*), **Banana**
bran (*right*).

OAT PANCAKES

MAKES 8 PANCAKES
Each pancake: 130 Cals, 3 g fat, 3 g fibre

50 g/2 oz 100% wholemeal flour
pinch salt
50 g/2 oz rolled oats
1 egg
15 g/½ oz brown sugar
275 ml/½ pint milk
15 ml/1 tbsp melted margarine or low-fat spread
4 apples
juice 1 lemon
45 ml/3 tbsp chopped dates

Stir together the flour, salt and rolled oats. In a separate bowl, beat together the egg, sugar, milk and melted butter. Stir in the flour and oats. Leave to stand for 30 minutes or, if more convenient, cover and leave overnight, then beat again before using.

Heat a non-stick omelette pan (lightly smear with a little oil, if necessary). When the pan is hot, pour on just enough pancake mixture to cover the base of the pan very thinly. Tip the pan to spread the mixture evenly and fry until it bubbles. Turn over and cook the other side until golden brown. Slide on to a warmed dish and keep warm while making the rest.

Core the apples, cut into slices and toss in the lemon juice. Divide the apples and dates between the pancakes and roll up. Serve hot.

RICH OATMEAL BISCUITS

MAKES 16 BISCUITS
Each biscuit: 110 Cals, 5 g fat, 1 g fibre

100 g/4 oz 100% wholemeal flour
pinch salt
5 ml/1 tsp baking powder
65 g/2½ oz margarine
175 g/6 oz medium or coarse oatmeal
40 g/1½ oz brown sugar
1 egg, lightly beaten

Heat the oven to 180°C/350°F/Gas 4. Grease a baking tray.

Sift together the flour, salt and baking powder and add any bran remaining in the sieve. Rub in the margarine until the mixture resembles fine breadcrumbs. Stir in the oatmeal and sugar and bind the mixture with the egg. Knead to a smooth dough.

Roll out on a lightly floured surface until 6 mm/¼ in thick and, using a 6.5-cm/2½-in cutter, cut out in rounds. Transfer to the baking tray and bake for 15–20 minutes, until golden brown and crisp. Allow to cool slightly, then transfer to a wire tray.

These are very good instead of toast, especially if eaten with fresh orange segments or dried fruit compôte (see page 28).

OATCAKES

MAKES 8 OATCAKES
Each oatcake: 220 Cals, 9 g fat, 3 g fibre

225 g/8 oz rolled oats
100 g/4 oz 100% wholemeal flour
2.5 ml/½ tsp salt
5 ml/1 tsp baking powder
50 g/2 oz margarine
cold water to mix

Heat the oven to 180°C/350°F/Gas 4. Grease a baking tray.

Mix together the rolled oats, flour, salt and baking powder. Rub in the margarine and mix with enough cold water to make a firm dough. Sprinkle some oats on to a lightly floured surface, turn out the dough and knead lightly. Roll out to about 6-mm/¼-in thickness. Cut into 8, transfer to the baking tray and bake for 25 minutes, until golden brown. Cool on the tray then transfer to a wire rack.

See photograph on p.25.

SPICED APPLE SCONES

SERVES 4

Per serving: 205 Cals, 11 g fat, 3 g fibre

75 g/3 oz 100% wholemeal flour
5 ml/1 tsp cream of tartar
2.5 ml/½ tsp salt
2.5 ml/½ tsp bicarbonate of soda
1 ml/¼ tsp ground cinnamon
30 ml/2 tbsp vegetable oil
1 egg
150 ml/5 fl oz milk
25 g/1 oz brown sugar
2 apples, cored and finely chopped

To serve:
low-fat cottage cheese and apple slices or orange segments

Sift together the flour, cream of tartar, salt, soda and cinnamon and add the bran remaining in the sieve. Beat in the oil and egg, then the milk and sugar.

Heat a heavy-based non-stick frying-pan or griddle (smear with a little oil if necessary). Stir the chopped apples into the batter and drop spoonfuls of the mixture well apart on to the hot surface and cook for 1 minute on each side, or until the scones are brown and bubbling.

Serve warm with low-fat cottage cheese and fresh apple slices or orange segments.

RYE CRISPBREAD

MAKES 20 CRISPBREADS

Each crispbread: 55 Cals, 2 g fat, 1 g fibre

225 g/8 oz rye flour
2.5 ml/½ tsp salt
50 g/2 oz margarine
30 ml/2 tbsp milk
30 ml/2 tbsp water

Heat the oven to 200°C/400°F/Gas 6. Grease 2–3 large baking trays.

Put the flour and salt into a bowl and rub in the margarine until the mixture resembles fine breadcrumbs. Pour on the milk and water and mix quickly to form a firm dough. Knead on a lightly floured surface until smooth, then roll to about 3 mm/⅛ in thick. Cut into 8-cm/3¼-in squares and transfer to the baking trays. Prick all over with a fork to prevent them rising.

Bake for 10–12 minutes, until the crispbreads just begin to colour at the edges. Do not let them brown. Allow to cool slightly on the baking trays before transferring to wire racks.

CRISPY BRAN CAKES WITH SCRAMBLED EGGS

SERVES 4
Per serving: 180 Cals, 8 g fat, 7 g fibre

150 ml/5 fl oz milk
5 eggs
75 g/3 oz All-Bran
25 g/1 oz 100% wholemeal flour
2.5 ml/½ tsp salt
a knob of margarine
ground black pepper
2 large tomatoes, skinned and chopped or 2 anchovies, chopped

Garnish:
4 sprigs parsley (optional)

Heat the oven to 220°C/425°F/Gas 7. Grease a baking tray.

To make the bran cakes, beat together the milk, 1 egg and the All-Bran – leave for about 10 minutes, until the liquid has been absorbed. Stir in the flour and salt. Divide into 4 and spread in circles on the baking tray. Bake for 20–25 minutes, until crisp.

Meanwhile, melt the margarine in a small pan. Beat the remaining eggs, season with salt and pepper and stir in the tomatoes or anchovies (omit the salt if anchovies are used). Cook the eggs over low heat, stirring with a wooden spoon.

Transfer the bran cakes to a warm serving dish, pile the egg mixture on top, garnish with the parsley, if liked, and serve at once.

GOOD MORNING SCONES

SERVES 4
Per serving: 270 Cals, 9 g fat, 7 g fibre

25 g/1 oz All-Bran
60 ml/4 tbsp milk, and extra to glaze
225 g/8 oz 81% wheatmeal self-raising flour (see page 108)
2.5 ml/½ tsp salt
25 g/1 oz butter
1 egg

Heat the oven to 220°C/425°F/Gas 7. Grease a baking tray.

Stir together the All-Bran and milk and leave for about 10 minutes, until the liquid has been absorbed. Stir together the flour, baking powder, if used, and salt and rub in the butter until the mixture resembles fine breadcrumbs.

Beat the egg into the soaked bran mixture, pour it on to the flour and stir quickly to form a dough.

Knead the dough lightly and shape into an 18-cm/7-in round. Lightly score the top into 8 sections and brush with milk. Place on the baking tray and bake for 10–12 minutes. Serve warm with cottage cheese and sultanas or raisins.

The dough can be made the evening before, and left ready to bake fresh for breakfast. Glaze the top just before baking.

Oatcakes (*left*, see p.22), Good morning scones (*top*), Crispy bran cakes with scrambled eggs (*right*).

OPEN SANDWICHES

Whether you make your own crispbread, buy packets of bran or other crispbreads, or use wholemeal bread, you will find open sandwiches very convenient for nourishing breakfasts that are quick to prepare and quick to eat. The fillings can be mixed, sliced, grated or chopped the night before, but do not put them on the biscuits until just before serving, or they will go limp.

Low-fat soft cheese combines well with many ingredients to give a whole range of suitable toppings. Try mixing it with fruit purées and top with fresh fruit, or try it with any of the following:

Chunky marmalade Top with orange segments.
Chopped dates and bananas Top with sliced apple dipped in lemon juice.
Sultanas or raisins Top with shredded coconut.
Finely chopped dried apricots Top with chopped walnuts.
Chopped dates and grated carrot Top with thinly sliced carrot 'pennies'.
Chopped mint Top with a row of orange segments.
Chopped apple and grated carrot Top with a little grated carrot.
Low-fat plain yoghurt and grated Edam cheese Add a pinch of cayenne pepper and top with sliced tomato.
Low-fat plain yoghurt and mashed banana Top with walnut or pecan halves.
Low-fat plain yoghurt and fresh pineapple Garnish with apple slices dipped in lemon juice.

POTATO HOTCAKES

SERVES 4
Per serving: 85 Cals, 3 g fat, 3 g fibre

1 kg/2 lb 4 oz potatoes, peeled or scraped
30 ml/2 tbsp 100% wholemeal flour
15 ml/1 tbsp bran
10 ml/2 tsp mustard powder
1 small onion, grated
salt and ground black pepper
2 eggs, beaten

Soak the potatoes in cold water for at least 30 minutes. Grate and discard any liquid. Stir in the flour, bran, mustard powder and onion, season with salt and pepper and then stir in the eggs. (You can prepare the mixture to this point overnight.)

Heat a heavy non-stick frying-pan (smear lightly with oil, if necessary). When the pan is hot, drop in spoonfuls of the mixture. When brown underneath, turn over and brown the other side.

Serving suggestion
Serve with grilled tomatoes, mushrooms, fish or low-fat cottage cheese.

POTATO CORNERS

SERVES 4
Per serving: 260 Cals, 6 g fat,
6 g fibre

500 g/1 lb potatoes, peeled or
scraped
salt
15 g/½ oz margarine
30 ml/2 tbsp milk
ground black pepper
100 g/4 oz canned sweetcorn,
drained
100 g/4 oz rolled oats

To serve:
grilled tomatoes and
mushrooms

Cook the potatoes in boiling, salted water for 15–20 minutes until tender. Drain and mash with the margarine and milk and season with salt and pepper. Stir in the sweetcorn and oats and knead to make a smooth dough. Turn on to a lightly floured surface and roll to 6-mm/¼-in thickness. Cut in triangles.

Heat a heavy non-stick frying-pan (smear lightly with oil, if necessary) and fry the triangles over a high heat, turning them over to brown both sides.

Serve hot with grilled tomatoes and mushrooms.

STUFFED MUSHROOMS

SERVES 4
Per serving: 245 Cals, 10 g
fat, 8 g fibre

8 large mushrooms
1 small onion, finely chopped
2 large tomatoes, halved
15 g/½ oz margarine
90 ml/6 tbsp wholemeal
breadcrumbs
40 g/1½ oz Cheddar cheese,
grated
50 g/2 oz canned sweetcorn,
drained
5 ml/1 tsp chopped mint
salt and ground black pepper
1 egg, beaten
4 slices wholemeal bread,
toasted

Heat the oven to 190°C/375°F/Gas 5. Grease a baking dish.

Chop the mushroom stalks and finely chop the onion. Scoop out the flesh from the tomatoes with a teaspoon. Melt the margarine in a pan and fry the mushroom stalks and onion over moderate heat for about 3 minutes, or until the onion is soft but not coloured. Remove from the heat and stir in the tomato flesh, breadcrumbs, cheese, sweetcorn and mint, season with salt and pepper and add just enough egg to bind together.

Arrange the mushrooms, stalk sides up, and the tomatoes, cut sides up, in the dish. Spoon the cheese mixture into the mushroom caps and on to the tomatoes, pressing well down. Cover with foil and bake for 20 minutes.

Serve hot on the toast.

PRUNE YOGHURT

SERVES 4
Per serving: 225 Cals, 1 g fat, 6 g fibre

225 g/8 oz prunes, soaked
30 ml/2 tbsp sultanas
425 ml/15 fl oz low-fat plain
   yoghurt
30 ml/2 tbsp lemon juice

Garnish:
a little All-Bran

Drain the prunes, halve them and remove the stones. Put in a bowl and stir in the sultanas, yoghurt and lemon juice. Cover and chill.

Serve sprinkled with All-Bran.

ORANGE SALAD

SERVES 4
Per serving: 195 Cals, 8 g fat, 6 g fibre

6 oranges
150 ml/5 fl oz low-fat cottage
   cheese
60 ml/4 tbsp low-fat plain
   yoghurt
50 g/2 oz blanched almonds,
   toasted

Grate the rind of 2 of the oranges and stir into the cottage cheese and yoghurt.

Segment the oranges and stir into the cheese mixture. Stir in most of the almonds, reserving a few for decoration. Cover and chill.

Scatter with the reserved almonds to serve.

DRIED FRUIT COMPÔTE

SERVES 4
Per serving: 108 Cals, 0 g fat, 10 g fibre

225 g/8 oz mixed dried fruits
   – apple rings, apricots, figs,
   peaches, pears, prunes –
   soaked overnight
grated rind and juice 1 lemon
150 ml/5 fl oz unsweetened
   apple juice
pinch cinnamon

Drain the fruit and measure 275 ml/½ pint of the soaking water into a pan; add the lemon rind and juice, apple juice, pinch of cinnamon and fruit. Bring slowly to the boil, cover and simmer for 30 minutes.

For those who like a hot breakfast, this compôte is delicious served steaming hot. But if it is to be served cold, chill and serve with low-fat plain yoghurt.

Prune yoghurt (*left*), **Orange salad** (*right*).

3 Soups, Snacks And Salads

Soups are the very essence of home cooking. As with all traditional farmhouse fare, they make the best of each season's ingredients and all the trimmings and left-overs, offering limitless variety at very low cost.

The best soups are those based on home-made stock which is simple to make from bones, root vegetables, herbs and spices. (Recipes for three basic stocks follow.)

The stocks themselves do not contain fibre, but they do give good, full flavour and body to the other ingredients – the vegetables, pulses, pasta and rice – you add. Bought stock cubes can be substituted, but they won't give such good results, and they are salty, so you will need to adjust the salt content of the recipe to suit your taste.

If possible, leave all vegetable skins on the soup ingredients to provide extra fibre.

An easy way to add fibre to soups is to stir in some bran.

You can add more fibre and contrasts of texture to soups with garnishes sprinkled on just before serving or handed round separately. Try chopped nuts, cooked pasta or toasted wholewheat breadcrumbs for instant toppings.

Or make a selection of garnishes to store – ideas on pages 42–3. Serve the high-fat ones such as fried croutons and 'buttered' crumbs sparingly.

Try to get used to the underlying basic method in the soup recipes: low in fat, they combine vegetables and stock without, in most cases, frying them first.

Perhaps it is in the area of snacks and light meals that we are most vulnerable. Even people conscientiously trying to eat sensibly are prone to make lack of time an excuse for snatching something quite unsuitable – a doughnut or a bar of chocolate, perhaps – when they really could do better.

Always use wholemeal products for snacks – not only are they higher in fibre, they have added flavour and are more filling – which can prevent nibbling at sweet or fatty foods.

As cooked dried pulses, wholemeal pastas and brown rice keep for several days in the refrigerator, try to cook a large amount so they will be available to provide a base for a snack or salad.

Salad dressings can be made from low-fat plain yoghurt or soft cheese and unsweetened fruit juices – lemon, apple, orange and tomato – with herbs and seasonings added for flavour.

It is easy to make your own low-fat soft cheese from yoghurt. Simply line a colander with a double layer of scalded muslin or tea towel, stand it in a bowl and pour in the yoghurt. Cover and leave to drain for 1 day. You can flavour the cheese with chopped herbs or crushed garlic – it makes a delicious sandwich spread.

If buying cottage, curd or other soft cheeses, make sure they are low fat.

Camembert and Edam have the least calories of the semi-hard or hard cheeses.

STOCKS

BASIC STOCKS

A soup can only be as good as the basic stock that is used. However convenient it may be at times, no stock cube can be expected to give your soups the home-made flavour that is achieved by boiling bones, vegetables and herbs, although these don't actually contribute any fibre. As stock can be kept for a week in the refrigerator, or frozen for longer storage, it is worth making several batches.

WHITE STOCK

MAKES APPROX 1.25 litres/2¼ pints

1 kg/2 lb 4 oz veal bones, or a chicken carcass
1 large onion, sliced
2 carrots, sliced
4 stalks celery, sliced
few stalks parsley
1 bay leaf
5 ml/1 tsp salt
6 black peppercorns

Put the bones in a large pan, pour on 2.25 litres/4 pints of water, cover and bring slowly to the boil. Skim off the scum that rises to the surface. Add the vegetables, salt and peppercorns. Cover, return to the boil and simmer for 3 hours, by which time the liquid should have reduced by about half. Strain carefully, and discard the ingredients. Allow to cool, then lift off the layer of fat. If you want to use the stock while it is hot, carefully skim off the fat that has risen to the surface.

Serving suggestions
Use for vegetable, poultry and some fruit soups.

VEGETABLE STOCK

MAKES ABOUT 1.25 litres/2¼ pints

2 large onions, sliced
2 large carrots, sliced
6 stalks celery, sliced
1 small turnip, sliced
1 large leek, sliced
bunch fresh herbs or a bouquet garni
5 ml/1 tsp salt
6 black peppercorns

Pour 2.25 litres/4 pints water into a large pan, add the vegetables, cover and bring to the boil. Skim off the scum as it rises. Add the herbs, salt and pepper, cover and return to the boil. Simmer for about 3 hours, or until the liquid has reduced by about half.

Finish as for white stock on page 31.

Serving suggestions
Use for vegetable and fruit soups if preferred to white stock, or whenever a vegetarian stock is required.

BROWN STOCK

MAKES ABOUT 1.25 litres/2¼ pints

1 kg/2 lb 4 oz beef bones
15 ml/1 tbsp beef dripping
1 large onion, sliced
2 carrots, sliced
4 stalks celery, sliced
bunch mixed fresh herbs or a bouquet garni
5 ml/1 tsp salt
6 black peppercorns

Put the bones in a large pan with the dripping and fry, turning occasionally, until brown on all sides. Add the vegetables and fry until light brown. Pour on 2.25 litres/4 pints water, cover, bring slowly to the boil and skim off the scum that rises to the surface. Add the herbs, salt and pepper, cover and return to the boil. Simmer for about 3 hours, or until reduced by about half.

Finish as for white stock on page 31.

Serving suggestions
Use for 'brown meat' soups, or to make clear soup.

SOUPS

ONION AND CARROT SOUP

SERVES 4
Per serving: 150 Cals, 6 g fat, 6 g fibre

15 ml/1 tbsp vegetable oil
500 g/1 lb onions, thinly sliced
1 litre/1¾ pints brown stock (see above)
225 g/8 oz carrots, grated
2.5 ml/½ tsp soft brown sugar
salt and ground black pepper
2 thick slices wholemeal bread
15–30 ml/1–2 tbsp grated Edam cheese

Heat the oil in a large pan, add the onions and sweat over medium heat for about 7–8 minutes, stirring occasionally. Pour on the stock, add the carrot and sugar and bring to the boil. Cover and simmer for 1 hour. Season with salt and pepper.

Heat the grill to high.

Cut the bread into triangles. Pour the soup into a heatproof serving bowl, float the bread on top and lightly sprinkle with cheese. Grill for 3–4 minutes until the cheese bubbles. Serve at once.

VEGETABLE SOUP

SERVES 4

Per serving: 40 Cals, 0 g fat, 3 g fibre

1 large onion, chopped
500 g/1 lb vegetables – such as parsnips, carrots, Jerusalem artichokes, courgettes, leeks – prepared and chopped
1 litre/1¾ pints white or vegetable stock (see pages 31–2)
salt and ground black pepper

Simmer the onion and vegetables in the stock, seasoned with salt and pepper, for 20 minutes, or until the vegetables are tender. Reduce to a purée in an electric blender or by rubbing through a sieve. Return to the rinsed pan and adjust the seasoning.

Serving suggestions
To increase the fibre content, stir in 30 ml/2 tbsp All-Bran just before serving the soup. The characteristic flavour of All-Bran goes particularly well with root vegetables. Or add a high-fibre garnish: wholemeal croûtons, cooked wholemeal pasta, cheese toasts, crumbs, crumbled bran crispbread and Bran Flakes all make tasty toppings (see page 42).

Alternative suggestions
Carrot and orange   Grate the rind and squeeze the juice of 1 large orange. Stir both rind and juice into the soup when you reheat it. Garnish the soup with a little grated raw carrot or with a small swirl of sour cream. In this case, serve matchsticks of raw carrot as an extra.

Cauliflower   Add 2.5 ml/½ tsp grated nutmeg to the cauliflower purée. Garnish with herb croûtons (see page 43).

Dried pea or bean   Use 225 g/8 oz dried peas, beans or lentils. Soak the pulses overnight, drain them and cook them in the stock for 1–3 hours according to type. Add a bunch of fresh herbs and a bay leaf, or a *bouquet garni* to the stock and discard before reducing to a purée. Garnish with chopped parsley, chives or mint.

Pea   Add 30 ml/2 tbsp chopped mint to the peas when cooking, and stir in the grated rind and squeezed juice of 1 lemon when you reheat the purée. When the peas are young and tender, you can make the soup with the topped-and-tailed pea pods and add a few cooked peas as a garnish.

PEARL BARLEY SOUP

SERVES 4

Per serving: 70 Cals,
negligible fat, 3 g fibre

75 g/3 oz pearl barley, soaked
and drained (see page 58)
1.4 litres/2½ pints white or
vegetable stock (see pages
31–2)
1 bay leaf
1 large onion, sliced
2 medium-sized carrots, diced
2 medium-sized potatoes, diced
salt and ground black pepper

Garnish:
15 ml/1 tbsp chopped dill or
parsley

Simmer the pearl barley, with the bay leaf, in the stock
in a large covered pan for 1½ hours. Add the vegetables,
season with salt and pepper and simmer for 30
minutes. Remove the bay leaf. Serve garnished with
the dill or parsley.

PASTA AND MUSHROOM SOUP

SERVES 4

Per serving: 70 Cals,
negligible fat, 3 g fibre

850 ml/1½ pints brown stock
(see page 32)
75 g/3 oz wholemeal pasta
shapes
2 stalks celery, thinly sliced
50 g/2 oz mushrooms, thinly
sliced
2 tomatoes, skinned and
quartered
salt and ground black pepper

Garnish:
15 ml/1 tbsp chopped mint

Bring the stock to the boil in a large pan and add the
pasta and celery. Return to the boil, cover and simmer
for about 13 minutes, or until the pasta is tender. Add
the mushrooms and tomatoes, season with salt and
pepper and simmer for 2 minutes. Sprinkle with the
chopped mint just before serving.

SOYA BEAN AND LEEK SOUP

SERVES 4
Per serving: 145 Cals, 5 g fat, 5 g fibre

100 g/4 oz soya beans, soaked and drained (see page 58)
1 small onion
4 cloves
1 bay leaf
2 large carrots, diced
4 small leeks, sliced
1.1 litre/2 pints brown stock (see page 32)
salt and ground black pepper

Garnish:
15 ml/1 tbsp chopped chives

Simmer the beans in a large covered pan, with the onion stuck with the cloves and the bay leaf, for 2½ hours. Drain and discard the liquid and other vegetables.

Return the beans to the rinsed pan with the carrots, leeks and stock and bring to the boil. Simmer for 1 hour, or until the beans are tender. Season with salt and pepper and serve garnished with chives.

CURRIED COURGETTE SOUP

SERVES 4
Each serving: 40 Cals, 0 g fat, 3 g fibre

500 g/1 lb courgettes, sliced
1 large onion
5 ml/1 tsp curry powder (or more to taste)
1 litre/1¾ pints white or vegetable stock (see pages 31–2)
salt and ground black pepper
60 ml/4 tbsp cooked brown rice

Garnish:
a few curried croûtons (see page 43)

Simmer the courgettes, onion, curry powder and stock in a large covered pan for 15–20 minutes, or until tender. Liquidize the vegetables and stock in a blender, purée in a food mill or pass them through a sieve.

Return to the rinsed pan and season with salt and pepper. Add the rice and heat through. Scatter the curried croûtons over just before serving, or serve separately.

WINTER SOUP

SERVES 4

Per serving: 56 Cals,
negligible fat, 4 g fibre

25 g/1 oz 100% wholemeal
   flour
15 ml/1 tbsp paprika
1 litre/1¾ pints white or brown
   stock (see pages 31–2)
2 large leeks, sliced
2 medium-sized carrots, diced
225 g/8 oz white cabbage,
   shredded
400 g/14 oz canned tomatoes
salt and ground black pepper

To serve:
2 slices cheese toasts (see page
   43) topped with parsley

Mix together the flour and paprika and gradually stir in a little of the stock to make a smooth paste. Bring the remaining stock to the boil. Stir a little into the paste, return to the pan and bring back to the boil, stirring. Add the leeks, carrots, cabbage and tomatoes, and season with salt and pepper. Cover and simmer for about 40 minutes, or until the vegetables are tender. Adjust the seasoning if necessary.

Serve with cheese toasts.

Alternative suggestion
Particularly if using brown stock as the base, you might like to make the soup even more substantial by serving tiny dumplings (see page 43) instead of cheese toasts. Add to the soup 10 minutes before the end of cooking time.

BEAN AND PASTA SOUP

SERVES 6

Per serving: 220 Cals, 2 g fat,
16 g fibre

100 g/4 oz shelled broad beans
   (shelled weight)
1 large onion, sliced
1.1 litre/2 pints brown stock
   (see page 32)
300 g/10 oz cooked dried red
   kidney beans
75 g/3 oz wholemeal pasta
   shapes
10 ml/2 tsp tomato purée
salt and ground black peper

Garnish:
15 ml/1 tbsp chopped parsley

Simmer the broad beans, onion and stock in a large covered pan for 10 minutes. Add the kidney beans, pasta and tomato purée, and boil for 13 minutes, or until the pasta is tender.

Garnish with the parsley.

Bean and pasta soup (*top*),
Winter soup (*centre*), Spiced
lentil soup (*bottom*, see p.38).

SPICED LENTIL SOUP

SERVES 4
Per serving: 180 Cals,
negligible fat, 7 g fibre

225 g/8 oz red lentils, washed
  and drained
1 large onion, sliced
1 bay leaf
2 stalks celery, thinly sliced
700 ml/1¼ pints brown stock
  (see page 32)
2.5 ml/½ tsp ground turmeric
2.5 ml/½ tsp ground ginger
salt and ground black pepper

Garnish:
a few herb croûtons (see page
  43) or a little All-Bran

Simmer the lentils, onion, bay leaf, celery and stock in a large, covered pan for 30–40 minutes until the lentils are soft. Discard the bay leaf. Stir in the turmeric and ginger, season with salt and pepper and beat with a wooden spoon.

This soup has a rough texture, but if a smoother one is required, liquidize in a blender, purée in a food mill or pass through a sieve.

Just before serving, add a very few herb croûtons, or a little All-Bran.

See photograph on p.37.

BORSCH

SERVES 4
Per serving: 90 Cals, 2 g fat,
5 g fibre

500 g/1 lb raw beetroots
1 large onion, chopped
110 g/4 oz cabbage, shredded
grated rind and juice 1 lemon
30 ml/2 tbsp tomato purée
1 litre/1¾ pints brown stock
  (see page 32)
1 bay leaf
few stalks of parsley
salt and ground black pepper
30 ml/2 tbsp sultanas

Garnish:
30 ml/2 tbsp soured cream

Thinly peel and grate the beetroots. In a large covered pan simmer the vegetables, lemon rind and juice, tomato purée, stock, bay leaf and parsley stalks, salt and pepper for 30–45 minutes, or until the vegetables are tender. Adjust the seasoning if necessary and discard the bay leaf and parsley stalks. Just before serving, stir in the sultanas and garnish with the soured cream.

BUTTER BEAN AND CARROT SOUP

SERVES 4
Per serving: 81 Cals,
negligible fat, 7 g fibre

100 g/4 oz dried butter beans,
soaked and drained (see
page 58)
225 g/8 oz carrots, chopped
1 small onion, sliced
850 ml/1½ pints white or
vegetable stock (see pages
31–2)
salt and ground black pepper
15 ml/1 tbsp chopped
coriander or parsley

Simmer the beans, carrots, onion and stock in a large, covered pan for 1¼–1½ hours, or until the beans are just tender.

Remove a few of the whole beans with a slotted spoon and set aside. Liquidize the remaining vegetables and the stock in a blender, purée in a food mill or pass through a sieve. Return to the rinsed pan and season with salt and pepper. Add the reserved whole beans and heat through. Serve garnished with the chopped herb.

KIDNEY BEAN SOUP

SERVES 4
Per serving: 160 Cals, 1 g fat,
15 g fibre

225 g/8 oz red kidney beans –
or others such as black-
eyed or pinto beans – soaked
and drained (see page 58)
1 medium-sized onion, sliced
few parsley stalks
1 bay leaf
850 ml/1½ pints brown stock
(see page 32)
2 stalks celery, chopped
1 medium-sized carrot,
chopped
salt and ground black pepper
15 ml/1 tbsp cider vinegar

Garnish:
15 ml/1 tbsp parsley

Simmer the beans, onion, parsley stalks, bay leaf and stock in a large, covered pan for 30 minutes.

Add the celery and carrot, return to the boil and simmer for a further 30–45 minutes, or until the beans and vegetables are tender. Discard the bay leaf and parsley stalks. Season with salt and pepper and stir in the vinegar. Sprinkle with the chopped parsley just before serving.

FISH AND CORN CHOWDER

SERVES 4
Per serving: 310 Cals, 5 g fat,
7 g fibre

*500 g/1 lb smoked cod (or a
    mixture of white and
    smoked cod or white fish)*
575 ml/1 pint water
2 rashers bacon, rinds removed
1 large onion, thinly sliced
*500 g/1 lb small whole
    potatoes, scrubbed*
2 large carrots, thickly sliced
*100 g/4 oz mushrooms, thinly
    sliced*
*100 g/4 oz canned sweetcorn,
    drained*
10 ml/2 tsp mustard powder
275 ml/½ pint milk
30 ml/2 tbsp chopped parsley

Garnish:
*45 ml/3 tbsp 'buttered' crumbs
    (see page 42)*

Put the fish in a pan, pour on the water, cover and slowly bring to the boil. Simmer for about 10 minutes, or until the fish is firm. Drain, reserving the stock. Skin the fish, remove any bones and flake into large pieces.

Fry the bacon in a large pan until the fat runs. Spoon off the excess fat. Add the onion slices, stir well and cook over moderate heat for about 3 minutes. Remove from the heat. Add the potatoes, carrots, mushrooms and sweetcorn. Gradually mix a little of the milk and the mustard to a smooth paste then stir in the remaining milk. Pour into the pan and strain in the reserved fish stock. Cover and simmer for about 20 minutes, or until the potatoes and carrots are just cooked. Add the fish and parsley and gently reheat. Serve sprinkled with 'buttered' crumbs.

POTATO AND LEEK SOUP

SERVES 4
Per serving: 40 Cals, 0 g fat,
3 g fibre

*2 large leeks, trimmed and
    chopped*
500 g/1 lb potatoes, chopped
1 small onion, sliced
*1 litre/1¾ pints white or
    vegetable stock (see page
    32)*
salt and ground black pepper
pinch ground coriander

Garnish:
*60 ml/4 tbsp low-fat plain
    yoghurt*
30 ml/2 tbsp chopped chives

Simmer the leeks in a large, covered pan with the potatoes, onion and stock for about 15–20 minutes, or until tender. Liquidize the vegetables and stock, purée in a food mill or pass through a sieve.

Return to the rinsed pan and season with salt, pepper and a pinch of ground coriander.

Mix together the yoghurt and chives and swirl into the soup just before serving.

Iced vegetable soup (*bottom*, see p.42), **Potato and leek soup** (*top left*), **Fish and corn chowder** (*top right*).

ICED VEGETABLE SOUP

SERVES 4

Per serving: 120 Cals, 5 g fat, 4 g fibre

500 g/1 lb 2 oz canned tomatoes, puréed
700 ml/25 fl oz white stock (see page 31)
100 g/4 oz wholemeal bread-crumbs
30 ml/2 tbsp red wine vinegar
30 ml/2 tbsp olive oil
45 ml/3 tbsp dry white wine
1 green pepper, thinly sliced
1 red pepper, thinly sliced
1 large onion, finely chopped
2 cloves garlic, crushed
½ small cucumber, diced
15 ml/1 tbsp chopped parsley
salt and ground black pepper

Garnish:
garlic croûtons (see page 43)
or sunflower seeds, both
optional

Mix the tomato purée with the white stock and stir in the breadcrumbs, vinegar, olive oil and wine. Stir in the vegetables and parsley and season well with salt and pepper. Chill in a covered container for at least 2 hours, or overnight.

Serve in chilled bowls garnished with garlic croûtons or sunflower seeds if liked.

See photograph on p.41.

TOPPINGS AND GARNISHES

To add texture, and fibre, to soups, especially creamy ones, the following 3 recipes can be sprinkled on top just before serving or handed round separately.

As they are only eaten in small amounts, they will not contribute much fat to the diet. They can be stored in an airtight container for about 2 months.

'BUTTERED' CRUMBS

1 recipe: 720 Cals, 27 g fat, 21 g fibre

25 g/1 oz margarine
575 ml/1 pint measure of wholemeal breadcrumbs

Melt the margarine in a frying-pan, add the crumbs and remove the pan from the heat. Turn the crumbs over and over until the fat is absorbed. Spread on baking trays and dry in the oven, turning occasionally, at 130°C/250°F/Gas ½ for about 1 hour, or until straw-coloured. Allow the crumbs to cool completely, then store in a lidded jar.

CROÛTONS

1 recipe: 720 Cals, 27 g fat, 21 g fibre

25 g/1 oz margarine
6 × 12-mm/½-in thick slices wholemeal bread cut from a large loaf.

Melt the margarine in a frying-pan. Cut the bread into cubes and, when the fat is hot, add it to the pan. Stir until the cubes are dry and evenly brown. Turn on to crumpled kitchen paper. Allow to cool completely before storing.

Herb croûtons   Add 15 ml/1 tbsp chopped fresh herbs to the bread cubes just before they are dry. Experiment with parsley, chervil, marjoram, mint, and so on, or use mixed fresh or dried herbs.

Garlic croûtons   Fry 2 crushed garlic cloves with the bread cubes.

Curried croûtons   Toss the bread cubes in 15 ml/1 tbsp curry powder before frying.

CHEESE TOASTS

SERVES 4
Per serving: 120 Cals, 4 g fat, 3 g fibre

2 × 4-cm/1½-in thick slices wholemeal bread cut from a large loaf
50 g/2 oz Edam cheese, grated

Cut the bread into cubes, spread on a grill rack and grill, turning over once or twice, until evenly toasted. Cover completely with the cheese and grill until the cheese melts and bubbles. Break up into cubes again and serve very hot, sprinkled on soup or handed round separately.

DUMPLINGS

SERVES 4
Per serving: 95 Cals, 6 g fat, 1 g fibre

50 g/2 oz 81% wheatmeal self-raising flour (see page 108)
pinch salt
25 g/1 oz shredded suet
approx 30–45 ml/2–3 tbsp water to mix

Mix together the flour, salt and suet and add just enough water to make a firm dough. Dust your hands with flour and shape the dumplings into small balls about the size of a large walnut. Roll the dumplings in flour and add to the simmering soup 10 minutes before serving. Cover the pan. The dumplings will first sink, then rise to the surface. Do not have the soup fast-boiling as this will break up the dumplings.

Flavourings:
5 ml/1 tsp chopped fresh parsley or other herb
2.5 ml/½ tsp dried herbs
2.5 ml/½ tsp caraway seeds – particularly with brown stock soups and those containing cabbage
25 g/1 oz grated Edam cheese – particularly with cauliflower soup
1 small onion, finely chopped and lightly cooked in a very small amount of margarine – particularly with winter vegetable soups

SNACKS

CRUDITÉS

Since fingers and flowerets of crisp, fresh vegetables can be served in so many appealing ways in high-fibre meals, it is worth taking a little trouble to present them attractively. The natural colours and varied shapes are a perfect garnish to pâtés and dips, soups and salads; and they are delicious just dipped in plain, low-fat yoghurt to which herbs and seasonings have been added, as a crisp and crunchy first course.

Choose only the freshest vegetables which are in perfect condition, and make a selection that has built-in colour contrast. And, of course, don't peel them unless absolutely necessary.

Carrots   Trim the tops and root ends. Scrub well, but do not peel, then cut into thick matchsticks. Or cut very thin slices. For a pretty effect, these slices can be cut into flower shapes with biscuit cutters or a scalloped apple corer.

Cauliflower   Cut into medium-sized or small flowerets for using as 'dip-sticks' for soft pâté or dips.

Celery   Cut into 10-cm/4-in lengths and, with a very sharp knife, make deep slits in one end, not quite reaching the centre. Soak in ice-cold water for about 2 hours, or until the cut ends curl. Or cut 5-cm/2-in strips to make little 'boats' to fill with a smooth pâté or dip.

Cucumber   To make little boats, cut into 5-cm/2-in slices. Cut these in halves lengthways, then scoop out the seeds. Fill the hollows, as for celery, with a smooth pâté or dip.

Or for dipping, cut thick matchstick lengths or 6-mm/¼-in thick slices. To give the skin a striped effect, draw the prongs of a large fork down the length to scoop out narrow channels.

Mushrooms   Trim the stalk and cut slices through the stalk and cap. If to be used for scooping up a dip, the slices will have to be thick.

Peppers   Trim off the tops, discard the white pith and seeds inside and cut through crossways to make rings. Or cut through in half lengthways and cut into thick matchstick strips.

Radishes   To make 'roses', trim off the roots and tops and, with a sharp knife, cut a deep cross in the top. Put in ice-cold water for about 2 hours until the top opens out.

To make 'fans,' trim and make a series of cuts along the length, like cutting a French loaf. Soak the radishes in ice-cold water.

Spring onions   To make 'umbrellas', trim off the roots, outer layers and green tops – the tops can be used, chopped, in salads. Make deep cuts from the top, as for celery. Soak in ice-cold water until the tops open out.

Crudités (*top*), **Chive and garlic dip** (*centre*, **see p.46**), **Yoghurt curd dip** (*bottom*, **see p.46**).

CHIVE AND GARLIC DIP

MAKES 275 ml/½ pint
One recipe: 150 Cals, 3 g fat,
trace fibre

275 ml/10 fl oz low-fat plain
  yoghurt, chilled
2 cloves garlic, crushed
salt to taste
30 ml/2 tbsp chopped chives

Garnish:
pinch cayenne pepper

Beat the yoghurt, then beat in the garlic, salt and most
of the chives. Season with a little cayenne pepper and
turn into a serving bowl. Garnish with a little cayenne
and the remaining chives. Serve chilled.

See photograph on p.44.

YOGHURT CURD DIP

MAKES 425 ml/15 fl oz
One recipe: 312 Cals, 11 g
fat, 1 g fibre

225 g/8 oz low-fat cottage
  cheese, sieved
150 ml/5 fl oz low-fat plain
  yoghurt, chilled
1 small onion, grated or finely
  minced
5 ml/1 tsp lemon juice
salt and ground black pepper
5 ml/1 tsp tomato purée

Beat together the cottage cheese and yoghurt. Beat in
the onion and lemon juice, then the salt, pepper and
tomato purée. Adjust seasoning if necessary. Serve
chilled.

See photograph on p.44.

AUBERGINE PÂTÉ

SERVES 4
Per serving: 100 Cals, 8 g fat,
5 g fibre

2 large aubergines
2 small onions, grated
15 ml/1 tbsp bran
30 ml/2 tbsp oil
salt and ground black pepper
juice 1 lemon
45 ml/3 tbsp chopped parsley

Garnish:
few black olives

Heat the oven to 180°C/350°F/Gas 4.
    Prick the skins of the aubergines, place on a baking
sheet and cook for about 30 minutes, turning once, or
until they are soft. Or grill under medium heat for
about 10 minutes turning often. Hold the aubergines
under cold running water and remove the skins.
    Mash the aubergine flesh with the onion, bran and
oil, with a fork, or purée in a blender. Season with salt,
pepper and lemon juice and stir in half the parsley.
Turn into a serving dish and garnish with the remaining
parsley and black olives.

Serving suggestions
This pâté can be served in any of the ways described
for chick pea salad (see page 55). Or you can spoon it
into 4 hollowed-out lemon shells. For a more substantial
dish, spoon into shells you can eat: hollow out large
tomatoes, pile the aubergine pâté into a dome shape
and put back the 'lids' at an angle.

ITALIAN TUNA TOMATOES

SERVES 4
Per serving: 320 Cals, 20 g fat, 6 g fibre

6 *large tomatoes*
15 *ml/1 tbsp vegetable oil*
1 *small onion, chopped*
1 *clove garlic, crushed*
100 *g/4 oz fresh wholemeal breadcrumbs*
15 *ml/1 tbsp bran*
200–225 *g/7–8 oz canned tuna fish, drained and flaked*
50 *g/2 oz can anchovies, finely chopped*
30 *ml/2 tbsp chopped parsley*
12 *stuffed green olives*
ground black pepper

Heat the oven to 190°C/375°F/Gas 5. Grease a baking dish.

Cut the tomatoes in halves crossways and scoop out most of the flesh, leaving firm 'walls'. Heat the oil in a pan and fry the onion and garlic over moderate heat for about 3 minutes, stirring once or twice. Remove from the heat and stir in the tomato flesh, breadcrumbs, bran, tuna, anchovies and parsley. Finely chop 9 of the olives, add to the pan and season with pepper. Pack into the tomato halves and place in the baking dish. Bake for 10–15 minutes, or until the top is crisp and brown. Chop the remaining olives and scatter on top to garnish.

Serving suggestion
Serve hot with wholemeal rolls.

PIZZA SCONE

SERVES 4
Per serving: 350 Cals, 20 g fat, 8 g fibre

Filling:
400 *g/14 oz canned tomatoes*
25 *g/1 oz bran*
1 *large onion, skinned and chopped*
1 *clove garlic, skinned and crushed*
2.5 *ml/½ tsp dried mixed herbs*
2.5 *ml/½ tsp dried oregano*
salt and ground black pepper
8 *stuffed green olives, sliced*

Base:
150 *g/6 oz 81% wheatmeal self-raising flour (see page 108)*
2.5 *ml/½ tsp baking powder*
50 *g/2 oz margarine*
90–105 *ml/6–7 tbsp milk*
75 *g/3 oz Edam cheese, grated*

Boil the tomatoes, bran, onion, garlic and herbs, seasoned with salt and pepper, for 5–7 minutes, until thickened to a spreadable consistency. Remove from the heat, check the seasoning and stir in the olives.

To make the scone base, stir together the flour and baking powder and rub in the margarine until the mixture resembles fine breadcrumbs. Add just enough milk to form a soft dough. Turn on to a lightly floured surface and knead until smooth. Shape into a 20-cm/8-in round.

Smear a 20-cm/8-in non-stick frying-pan with oil and slide the dough round into it. Cover the pan with a lid or foil and cook gently over low heat for about 10–20 minutes, or until well risen. Spread the tomato mixture on top and sprinkle with the cheese. Cook under a hot grill for 4–5 minutes, or until the cheese is golden brown and bubbling. Serve very hot, straight from the pan.

SALADS

COURGETTE AND BLACK BEAN SALAD

SERVES 4
Per serving: 220 Cals, 8 g fat,
13 g fibre

150 ml/5 fl oz low-fat plain
  yoghurt
15 ml/1 tbsp sunflower oil
15 ml/1 tbsp cider vinegar
salt and ground black pepper
4 small courgettes, thinly sliced
175 g/6 oz cooked dried black
  beans
2 spring onions, sliced
25 g/1 oz cashew nuts

Mix together the yoghurt, oil and vinegar and season with salt and plenty of pepper.

Stir together the courgettes, beans, onions and nuts. Toss in the dressing, cover and chill for at least 30 minutes.

MUNCHY PASTA SALAD

SERVES 4
Per serving: 260 Cals, 9 g fat,
5 g fibre

100 g/4 oz wholemeal pasta
  shapes, e.g. spaghetti rings
salt
15 ml/1 tbsp vegetable oil
15 ml/1 tbsp cider vinegar
3 apples
15 ml/1 tbsp lemon juice
4 stalks celery, thinly sliced
30 ml/2 tbsp raisins
30 ml/2 tbsp stoned dates,
  roughly chopped
30 ml/2 tbsp walnuts, roughly
  chopped
ground black pepper
15 ml/1 tbsp low-fat plain
  yoghurt, chilled
15 ml/1 tbsp soured cream,
  chilled
15 ml/1 tbsp unsweetened
  orange juice, chilled

Cook the pasta in a large pan in plenty of boiling, salted water for 12–13 minutes, or according to the directions on the packet, until just tender. Drain throroughly and toss, while still hot, with the oil and vinegar.

Core and thinly slice the apples and toss them in the lemon juice. Stir in the celery, raisins, dates and walnuts, mix well, then toss in the cooked pasta. Mix together the yoghurt, soured cream and orange juice, season with salt and pepper, and pour over the salad. Toss to blend thoroughly.

Cauliflower and bean salad (*above*, **see p.50**), **Munchy pasta salad** (*below*).

CAULIFLOWER AND BEAN SALAD

SERVES 4
Per serving: 170 Cals, 1 g fat,
15 g fibre

100 g/4 oz red kidney beans,
soaked and drained (see
page 58)
100 g/4 oz flageolets or haricot
beans, soaked and drained
(see page 58)
1 small cauliflower, in small
flowerets
150 ml/5 fl oz low-fat plain
yoghurt
15 ml/1 tbsp wine vinegar or
lemon juice
30 ml/2 tbsp grated horseradish
1 small clove garlic, crushed
10 ml/2 tsp bran
salt and ground black pepper
1 small onion, finely chopped

Cook the beans separately in unsalted water for 1 hour until tender. Meanwhile, steam the cauliflower for about 5–7 minutes until barely tender.

Shake or whisk together the yoghurt, vinegar, horseradish and bran, and season with salt and pepper. When the beans are cooked, drain and toss with the cauliflower and, while still hot, toss them in the dressing. Turn into a serving bowl and garnish with the parsley and lemon wedges.

See photograph on p.49.

Garnish:
15 ml/1 tbsp chopped parsley
lemon wedges

MIXED SALAD PLATE

SERVES 6
Per serving: 135 Cals, 1 g fat,
6 g fibre

700 g/1½ lb small new
potatoes, washed
salt
4 tomatoes, quartered
1 small cucumber, diced
2 stalks celery, chopped
1 green pepper, chopped
225 g/8 oz cooked broad beans
(fresh, frozen or canned)
100 g/4 oz cooked sliced green
beans
100 g/4 oz mushrooms, sliced
30 ml/2 tbsp chopped parsley
150 ml/5 fl oz low-fat plain
yoghurt
15 ml/1 tbsp lemon juice
15 ml/1 tbsp French mustard
salt and ground black pepper
30 ml/2 tbsp chopped chives

Cook the potatoes in boiling, salted water for about 15 minutes, or until just tender.

Beat together the yoghurt, lemon juice and mustard and season with salt and pepper. Pour two-thirds of the dressing over the mixed salad. Stir the chives into a third of the dressing and pour over the potatoes while still hot. Leave to cool. Mix together the tomatoes, cucumber, celery, pepper, broad beans, green beans, mushrooms and parsley. Pour over the remaining dressing. Spoon in a ring round the outside of a serving dish and pile the potatoes in the centre.

CELERIAC AND MUSHROOM SALAD

SERVES 4
Per serving: 120 Cals, 3 g fat,
5 g fibre

500 g/1 lb celeriac, scrubbed
  and trimmed
salt
30 ml/2 tbsp lemon juice
150 ml/5 fl oz low-fat plain
  yoghurt, chilled
15 ml/1 tbsp low-fat soft cheese
ground black pepper
pinch grated nutmeg
15 ml/1 tbsp chopped parsley
175 g/6 oz button mushrooms,
  thinly sliced

Garnish:
15 ml/1 tbsp toasted almonds

Cook the celeriac for about 20 minutes in boiling, salted water with half the lemon juice. Drain and leave to cool.

Mix together the yoghurt, cheese and remaining lemon juice. Season with pepper, salt and nutmeg and stir in the parsley.

Slice the celeriac very thinly, then cut into matchstick strips. Toss with the mushrooms, pour over the dressing and toss to blend thoroughly. Garnish with the toasted almonds.

Serving suggestions
This creamy-brown salad contrasts well with deep-green salad leaves such as spinach, sorrel or watercress. It can also be served as a side dish with roast or cold meats.

Alternative suggestions
Other 'white' root vegetables can be served in the same way – parsnips, turnips and seakale all make delicious salads. Very young root vegetables can be grated or thinly sliced and eaten raw – toss in lemon juice immediately to prevent discoloration, then in the yoghurt dressing.

FENNEL AND WALNUT SALAD

SERVES 4
Per serving: 175 Cals, 10 g
fat, 4 g fibre

4 bulbs of fennel, trimmed
salt
30 ml/2 tbsp lemon juice
15 ml/1 tbsp unsweetened
  orange juice
15 ml/1 tbsp oil
10 ml/2 tsp dry vermouth
ground black pepper
50 g/2 oz walnuts, chopped
1 small lettuce, shredded

Boil the fennel in salted water and lemon juice for 5 minutes. Drain thoroughly. Slice thinly into rings. Stir or beat together the lemon juice, orange juice, oil and vermouth and season with salt and pepper. Stir in the chopped walnuts and toss in the fennel.

Just before serving, arrange the lettuce around the outside of a serving dish and pile the fennel in the centre.

BROWN RICE FRUIT SALAD

SERVES 4
Per serving: 375 Cals, 9 g fat,
6 g fibre

225 g/8 oz brown long-grain
  rice
salt
2 apples
15 ml/1 tbsp lemon juice
8 prunes, soaked
2 oranges, peeled and
  segmented
15 ml/1 tbsp sunflower seeds
15 ml/1 tbsp vegetable oil
60 ml/4 tbsp low-fat plain
  yoghurt
15 ml/1 tbsp clear honey
30 ml/2 tbsp unsweetened
  apple juice
ground black pepper

Cook the rice in plenty of boiling, salted water for 30–40 minutes, or until just tender. Drain in a colander, refresh in cold, running water and drain thoroughly.

Core and thinly slice the apples and toss in lemon juice. Drain, halve and stone the prunes and cut into quarters. Toss together the rice, fruit and sunflower seeds.

To make the dressing, mix or shake together the oil, yoghurt, honey and apple juice and season with salt and pepper. Just before serving, pour the dressing over the salad and toss to coat the rice and fruit thoroughly. Garnish with the walnut halves.

Garnish:
walnut halves

DATE CHEESE SALAD

SERVES 4
Per serving: 210 Cals, 13 g
fat, 4 g fibre

100 g/4 oz low-fat cottage
  cheese, sieved
100 g/4 oz stoned dates,
  chopped
few drops vanilla essence
4 heads chicory, trimmed
  and sliced
1 bunch watercress, trimmed
60 ml/4 tbsp unsweetened
  orange juice
45 ml/3 tbsp vegetable oil
10 ml/2 tsp bran
5 ml/1 tsp sesame seeds
salt and ground black pepper

Mix together the cottage cheese and dates and add 2 or 3 drops of vanilla essence. Line 4 individual bowls with the chicory then the watercress and spoon a mound of the date mixture into the middle.

Mix or shake together the orange juice, oil, bran and sesame seeds and season with salt and pepper. Just before serving, spoon a little over the chicory and watercress and serve the rest separately.

Serving suggestions
As well as being a refreshing first course, this salad is a good accompaniment to barbecued or tandoori chicken, grilled steak or veal chops. Small amounts left can be piled into hollowed-out tomatoes to make a colourful first course or part of a mixed salad plate.

Soya bean and beansprout salad (*top*, see p.54), **Brown rice fruit salad** (*centre*), **Date cheese salad** (*bottom*).

Soya Bean and Beansprout Salad

SERVES 4

Per serving: 235 Cals, 9 g fat, 4 g fibre

grated rind and juice 1 orange
150 ml/5 fl oz low-fat plain
* yoghurt*
salt and ground black pepper
175 g/6 oz cooked soya beans
100 g/4 oz fresh beansprouts
1 small onion, sliced into rings
1 red pepper, thinly sliced

Stir the orange rind and juice into the yoghurt and season with salt and pepper. Toss together the beans, beansprouts, onion rings and pepper. Toss in the dressing, cover and chill. Serve garnished with the mint.

See photograph on p.52.

Garnish:
15 ml/1 tbsp chopped mint

Brown Lentil Salad

SERVES 4

Per serving: 170 Cals, 1 g fat, 7 g fibre

175 g/6 oz whole brown lentils
1 bay leaf
2 small onions
2 cloves
1 stalk celery, halved
30 ml/2 tbsp chopped mint
150 ml/5 fl oz low-fat plain
* yoghurt*
salt and ground black pepper
50 g/2 oz button mushrooms,
* thinly sliced*

Simmer the lentils with the bay leaf, one of the onions stuck with the cloves, and the celery in plenty of water in a covered pan for 40–45 minutes, or until tender. Drain and discard the bay leaf, onion, cloves and celery. Leave to cool.

Stir together the mint and yoghurt and season with salt and pepper. Slice the remaining onion into rings. Stir together the lentils, onion rings and mushrooms and stir in the yoghurt dressing. Turn into a serving dish and garnish with the tomatoes.

Garnish:
2 tomatoes, sliced

Two-bean and Leek Salad

SERVES 4

Per serving: 140 Cals, 1 g fat, 12 g fibre

150 ml/5 fl oz low-fat plain
* yoghurt*
5 ml/1 tsp tomato purée
5 ml/1 tsp cider vinegar
salt and ground black pepper
4 small, young leeks, trimmed
* and sliced*
1 small onion, sliced
75 g/3 oz cooked dried red
* kidney beans*
75 g/3 oz cooked dried haricot
* beans*

Mix together the yoghurt, tomato purée and vinegar and season with salt and pepper. Mix together the vegetables and beans and toss in the dressing. Cover and chill. Sprinkle with the parsley to serve.

Alternative suggestion
Salads are a wonderful way of using small amounts of ready-cooked pulses. Others can be used instead: chick peas, soya beans or mung beans, for example. And celery, onions or shallots could replace the leeks.

Garnish:
15 ml/1 tbsp chopped parsley

54

CHICK PEA SALAD (HUMMUS)

SERVES 4
Per serving: 340 Cals, 15 g fat, 9 g fibre

225 g/8 oz dried chick peas, soaked and drained (see page 58)
2.5 ml/½ tsp salt
10 ml/2 tsp ground cumin
45 ml/3 tbsp olive oil
75 ml/5 tbsp lemon juice
2 large cloves garlic, crushed
ground black pepper

Garnish:
30 ml/2 tbsp chopped parsley
lemon wedges

Boil the chick peas in unsalted water for 2–3 hours until tender. Add the salt and ground cumin towards the end of the cooking. Reserving a few peas to garnish, purée the rest with a little of the cooking water in an electric blender, food mill, or pass through a sieve. Beat or blend in the olive oil, lemon juice and garlic and season well with pepper.

Turn into a serving bowl and garnish with parsley, the reserved chick peas and the lemon wedges.

Serving suggestions
This creamy salad, which has the consistency of a dip, can be served in the traditional Middle-Eastern way, with hot pitta bread, or with fingers of hot wholemeal toast.

As an appetizer to serve with drinks, spread on small squares of rye bread, pumpernickel, or bran biscuits, and garnish with chopped parsley and black olive halves. Or serve in a small bowl surrounded by crudités (see page 45). Or spoon the hummus into celery 'boats' (see page 45) and sprinkle with a pinch of chopped parsley.

WHOLE CHICK PEA SALAD

SERVES 4
Per serving: 430 Cals, 18 g fat, 19 g fibre

225 g/8 oz dried chick peas, soaked and drained (see page 58)
2.5 ml/½ tsp salt
10 ml/2 tsp ground cumin
60 ml/4 tbsp oil
15 ml/1 tbsp Worcestershire sauce
30 ml/2 tbsp lemon juice
60 ml/4 tbsp tomato juice
10 ml/2 tsp bran
1 clove garlic, crushed
ground black pepper
2 small onions, sliced in rings

Garnish:
30 ml/2 tbsp chopped parsley

Cook the chick peas (see page 58). Add the salt and ground cumin just before the peas are cooked, then drain.

Mix together the Worcestershire sauce, lemon juice, tomato juice, bran and garlic and season with salt and pepper. Pour over the chick peas, add the onion rings, toss well, turn into a serving dish and garnish with the parsley.

Serving suggestions
This salad contrasts well with a green salad of lettuce, spinach or Chinese leaves scattered with finely chopped chives. It can also be served as an accompaniment to the main course and is especially good with smooth dishes such as vegetable soufflés and creamy vegetable casseroles.

CRACKED WHEAT SALAD

SERVES 4
Per serving: 160 Cals, 9 g fat, 5 g fibre

100 g/4 oz cracked wheat (burghul)
2 large spring onions, thinly sliced
45 ml/3 tbsp chopped mint
30 ml/2 tbsp chopped parsley
15 ml/1 tbsp chopped chervil
30 ml/2 tbsp olive oil
30 ml/2 tbsp lemon juice
salt and ground black pepper
a few lettuce leaves

Garnish:
30 ml/2 tbsp black olives
2 large tomatoes, quartered

Soak the cracked wheat in cold water for about 1 hour, or until it has 'exploded', then drain. Turn the wheat into a clean tea towel and wring the cloth from each end to expel the excess moisture – soggy cracked wheat is not pleasant.

Transfer the wheat to a bowl and stir in the onions, herbs, olive oil and lemon juice and season well with salt and pepper.

Line a serving dish with lettuce leaves and pile the salad on top. Garnish with the olives and tomato segments arranged in a design.

Serving suggestions
Serve with hot pitta bread or wholemeal rolls and matchsticks of fresh vegetables (see page 45).

MELON AND BEAN SALAD

SERVES 4
Per serving: 250 Cals, 8 g fat, 16 g fibre

1 honeydew melon
225 g/8 oz fresh beansprouts
1 clove garlic, crushed
1 small red pepper, thinly sliced
400 g/14 oz cooked dried red kidney beans
2 spring onions, sliced
50 g/2 oz cashew nuts
15 ml/1 tbsp chopped parsley
150 ml/5 fl oz low-fat plain yoghurt, chilled
5 ml/1 tsp lemon juice
grated rind and juice 1 orange
salt and ground black pepper

Garnish:
sprigs of watercress or parsley

Cut the melon in half and scoop out the seeds. Using a grapefruit knife with a curved blade, scoop out the melon flesh, then dice it. Or, with a fruit balling tool, scoop the melon flesh into balls. Mix the melon with the beansprouts, garlic, red pepper, kidney beans, spring onions, nuts and parsley. Put the salad to chill in the refrigerator.

Mix together the yoghurt, lemon juice and orange rind and juice. Season with salt and pepper, pour over the salad and toss well. Garnish with watercress or parsley sprigs.

BROWN RICE SALAD

SERVES 4
Per serving: 330 Cals, 11 g fat, 2 g fibre

225 g/8 oz brown long-grain rice
salt
2 spring onions
1 red pepper, sliced
2 stalks celery, sliced
50 g/2 oz stoned dates, chopped
25 g/1 oz blanched almonds, toasted
25 g/1 oz sunflower seeds
30 ml/2 tbsp vegetable oil
30 ml/2 tbsp unsweetened apple juice
30 ml/2 tbsp cider vinegar
10 ml/2 tsp bran
5 ml/1 tsp curry powder
1 clove garlic, crushed
ground black pepper

Cook the rice in plenty of boiling, salted water for 30–40 minutes, or until just tender. Drain in a colander and refresh in cold, running water. Drain thoroughly and leave to cool.

Toss together the rice, vegetables, dates, almonds and sunflower seeds.

Mix or shake together the oil, apple juice, vinegar, bran, curry powder and garlic and season with salt and pepper.

Just before serving, pour the dressing over the salad and toss thoroughly.

Serving suggestions
Dress up the salad by serving piled into grapefruit shells.

This salad makes a good accompaniment to kebabs, grilled meat or baked vegetable and cheese dishes.

SEAFOOD SALAD

SERVES 4
Per serving: 295 Cals, 6 g fat, 8 g fibre

225 g/8 oz wholemeal pasta shapes
salt
15 ml/1 tbsp vegetable oil
15 ml/1 tbsp cider vinegar
juice and rind 1 lemon
ground black pepper
225 g/½ lb cooked smoked haddock fillet, skinned and flaked
30 ml/2 tbsp capers, drained
30 ml/2 tbsp cooked peas
2 stalks celery, thinly sliced
100 g/4 oz sweetcorn
150 ml/5 fl oz low-fat plain yoghurt
30 ml/2 tbsp chopped parsley

Cook the pasta in a large pan of boiling, salted water for 12–13 minutes, or according to the directions on the packet, until just tender. Drain thoroughly. Mix or shake together the oil, vinegar and lemon juice. Season with salt and pepper and stir into the pasta while still hot.

Mix together the haddock, capers, peas, celery, sweetcorn and lemon rind. Stir in the yoghurt, then gently mix in the pasta shells, taking care not to break up the salad ingredients.

Turn the salad into a serving dish and sprinkle the parsley in a circle around the outside.

Serving suggestion
Tomato salad with chopped onion and fresh herbs, and wholemeal bread rolls.

Alternative suggestions
Pasta salads can be made to accommodate small amounts of other cooked fish – cod or smoked mackerel, for example – and cold, cooked chicken or turkey.

4 VEGETABLE DISHES

More and more people are discovering that vegetables need not be just a plain accompaniment to meat and fish dishes, but can be used in a wide variety of interesting ways – as a medley of vegetables, teamed with pastry, pancakes, wholemeal pasta, wholegrains or brown rice – and can actually provide the main course itself.

Pulses, the seeds of leguminous plants – peas, beans and lentils – are not only the highest of all in fibre but are cheap and readily available all year round.

For a perfect dietary balance, all pulses (except soya beans) should be combined with seeds, nuts, grains, wholemeal flour (in bread, pasta, and so on) or low-fat dairy produce.

Dried pulses (except lentils and split peas) need pre-soaking. Either bring them to the boil in a large pan of unsalted water, boil for 3–5 minutes, according to type, turn off the heat and leave to soak for at least 1 hour. Or soak them in three times their volume of cold water for 4–6 hours or overnight.

Cook pulses in the soaking water to retain the vitamins. But with them you retain the gases that can cause flatulence. If this is a problem, pour away the water and cook the pulses in fresh water or stock.

The cooking time for dried pulses varies according to the type and even the age – though you can't know how long they have been on the shelf. Allow from 30 minutes for lentils to 4 hours for chick peas and soya beans.

Wholemeal pasta and vegetables go well together. Pasta itself is not fattening – it contains about 208 calories for 50 g/2 oz raw weight. The calories mount up when it's served with butter, cream and egg sauces and a lot of hard cheese.

Wholemeal pasta and brown rice have more flavour and a firmer texture than their refined counterparts, but take a little longer to cook – pasta, 12–13 minutes generally; brown rice, up to 40 minutes, although some types have a cooking time of 25 minutes (always follow instructions on the packet). And because of the extra fibre they contain, they help you to feel satisfied for longer.

Don't peel vegetables, unless absolutely necessary, as the skins provide extra fibre.

BAKED JACKET POTATOES

SERVES 4
Per serving: 290 Cals, 9 g fat,
9 g fibre

4 large potatoes
15 ml/1 tbsp All-Bran
45 ml/3 tbsp milk
25 g/1 oz margarine
salt and ground black pepper
1 canned pimento, chopped
175 g/6 oz canned sweetcorn,
    drained
30 ml/2 tbsp chopped parsley
30 ml/2 tbsp grated Cheddar
    cheese

Heat the oven to 190°C/375°F/Gas 5.
Scrub the potatoes and prick the skins with a fork.
Place on a baking tray and bake for 1–1¼ hours, or until soft inside.
Meanwhile soak the All-Bran in the milk for 10 minutes.
Cut the cooked potatoes in halves and scoop out the flesh. Beat the potato with margarine, then beat in the milk mixture and season well with salt and pepper. Stir in the pimento, sweetcorn and parsley. Pile into the potato shells, sprinkle with the cheese and return to the oven for 10 minutes, until heated through.

Serving suggestions
The creamy white potato filling contrasts well with a green leaf vegetable such as spinach, with mixed green salad, tomato and onion salad, or matchsticks of raw root vegetables.

Alternative suggestions
For a crisp tasty filling, cook 175 g/6 oz broccoli spears or cauliflower flowerets until barely tender. Slice thickly and stir into the potato mixture with an extra 25 g/1 oz grated cheese.

CARROT SOUFFLÉ

SERVES 4
Per serving: 225 Cals, 14 g
fat, 5 g fibre

500 g/1 lb carrots, sliced
salt
50 g/2 oz margarine
50 g/2 oz wholemeal flour
275 ml/½ pint skimmed milk,
    warm (or half milk, half
    vegetable stock, from
    cooking carrots)
3 egg whites
1 egg yolk
ground black pepper
30 ml/2 tbsp chopped mint
25 ml/1 oz Edam cheese,
    grated

Heat the oven to 190°C/375°F/Gas 5. Grease a 1-litre/2-pint soufflé dish.
Steam or cook the carrots in boiling, salted water until tender. Drain and mash, reserving 150 ml/5 fl oz of the stock for the sauce, if liked.
Melt the margarine in a pan, stir in the flour and cook for 1 minute. Gradually stir in the milk and stock, if used. Bring to the boil. Simmer for 3 minutes, still stirring. Remove from the heat and beat in the egg yolk, carrot purée, salt, pepper and mint.
Whisk the egg whites until stiff and fold into the carrot mixture, using a metal spoon.
Turn into the soufflé dish and sprinkle with the cheese. Stand on a baking tray and bake for 45 minutes, or until well risen and golden brown. Serve at once.

Alternative suggestion
Cook, then purée 100 g/4 oz whole brown lentils and add to the sauce with 15 ml/1 tbsp each summer savory and parsley and a pinch of coriander in place of the carrots and mint.

BROCCOLI AND MACARONI CASSEROLE

SERVES 4
Per serving: 340 Cals, 3 g fat, 10 g fibre

225 g/8 oz wholemeal
macaroni
salt
500 g/1 lb broccoli
400 g/14 oz canned tomatoes
1 large onion, chopped
1 clove garlic, crushed
5 ml/1 tsp dried oregano
ground black pepper
275 ml/10 fl oz low-fat plain
yoghurt
100 g/4 oz low-fat soft cheese
30 ml/2 tbsp Bran Flakes

Garnish:
a sprig of parsley

Cook the macaroni in plenty of boiling, salted water for 12–13 minutes, or according to the directions on the packet, until just tender. Drain and keep warm.

Trim the broccoli and steam or cook in boiling, salted water, until just tender. Drain.

Simmer the tomatoes, onion, garlic and oregano, seasoned with salt and pepper, for 20 minutes, or until the onion is tender.

Heat the oven to 200°C/400°F/Gas 6.

Put a layer of the tomato sauce into an ovenproof dish, cover with a layer of cooked macaroni then a layer of broccoli. Repeat the layers.

Beat together the yoghurt and cheese, and season with salt and pepper. Spread over the casserole and bake for about 30 minutes, until the topping is bubbling and golden brown. Sprinkle with Bran Flakes, garnish with the parsley and serve very hot.

PASTA FLORENTINE

SERVES 4
Per serving: 355 Cals, 10 g fat, 18 g fibre

225 g/8 oz wholemeal short-
cut macaroni
salt
700 g/1½ lb fresh spinach
275 ml/10 fl oz low-fat plain
yoghurt
2 eggs
50 g/2 oz Edam cheese, grated
30 ml/2 tbsp bran
ground black pepper
pinch grated nutmeg

Garnish:
a little chopped parsley

Cook the macaroni in plenty of boiling, salted water for 12–13 minutes, or according to the directions on the packet, until just tender. Drain and keep warm.

Thoroughly wash the spinach and discard the tough centre stalks. Put the spinach in a large pan with just the water that clings to the leaves. Sprinkle on a large pinch of salt, cover and cook over moderate heat, shaking occasionally, for 10–15 minutes, until the spinach has collapsed and is tender. Drain thoroughly in a colander or sieve, pressing down firmly to remove all excess moisture.

Heat the oven to 200°C/400°F/Gas 6.

Beat together the yoghurt, eggs, cheese and bran and season with salt, pepper and nutmeg.

Grease a 1.5-litre/2½-pint ovenproof dish and spread the macaroni over the base. Spread the spinach over the pasta and pour on the sauce. Stand the dish on a baking tray and bake for 20–25 minutes, until the topping is deep brown and bubbling. Garnish with the parsley and serve very hot.

Serving suggestion
A tomato salad with thinly sliced onion rings makes a good accompaniment, contrasting with the main dish in both colour and texture.

Pasta Florentine (*above*),
Broccoli and macaroni casserole (*below*).

61

VEGETABLE LASAGNE

SERVES 4

Per serving: 405 Cals, 18 g fat, 5 g fibre

100 g/4 oz wholemeal lasagne
salt
100 g/4 oz whole brown lentils, washed and drained

Tomato sauce:
15 ml/1 tbsp vegetable oil
15 g/½ oz margarine
1 medium-sized onion, chopped
1 clove garlic, crushed
400 g/14 oz canned tomatoes
15 ml/1 tbsp tomato purée
ground black pepper
10 ml/2 tsp dried oregano

Topping:
25 g/1 oz margarine
25 g/1 oz 100% wholemeal flour
425 ml/15 fl oz milk
2 eggs, beaten
pinch grated nutmeg

Cook the lasagne in plenty of boiling, salted water for 13–14 minutes, or according to the directions on the packet, until just tender. Drain thoroughly and spread each piece separately to dry on a clean tea towel or on kitchen paper.

Cook the lentils in boiling water for 45–50 minutes, or until soft. Add salt just before the end of the cooking time. Drain any excess water.

Meanwhile, make the tomato sauce: heat the oil and margarine together in a pan, fry the onion and garlic over moderate heat for about 3 minutes without allowing the vegetables to brown. Add the tomatoes, stir well and simmer for about 30 minutes, or until the sauce thickens. Add the tomato purée and drained, cooked lentils. Season with salt and pepper, stir in the oregano and cook for about 5 minutes.

Grease a 1.5-litre/2½-pint ovenproof dish. Spoon in a layer of tomato and lentil sauce, cover with lasagne and repeat the layers, finishing with the sauce.

Heat the oven to 200°C/400°F/Gas 6.

To make the topping, melt the margarine in a small pan. Stir in the flour and cook for 1 minute. Gradually stir in the milk, bring to the boil and cook, stirring, for 3 minutes. Gradually beat the sauce on to the beaten eggs, and season with salt, pepper and nutmeg. Pour over the dish and push a knife down through the lasagne and sauce layers to allow the topping to seep through. Stand the dish on a baking tray and bake for 50–60 minutes, until the topping is deep brown and bubbling. Serve very hot.

SPAGHETTI WITH STIR-FRIED VEGETABLES

SERVES 6

Per serving: 320 Cals, 6 g fat, 3 g fibre

400 g/14 oz wholemeal spaghetti
15 g/1 tbsp vegetable oil
1 large onion, sliced
2 small leeks, thinly sliced
1 large carrot, thinly sliced
1 clove garlic, finely chopped
1 piece preserved ginger, washed and thinly sliced
few drops soy sauce
45 ml/3 tbsp dry sherry
salt and ground black pepper

Cook the spaghetti in a large pan in plenty of boiling, salted water for 12–13 minutes, or according to the directions on the packet, until just tender. Drain and keep warm.

In a large pan, heat the oil, then add the onion and stir over moderate heat for 2 minutes. Add the leeks and carrots and continue stirring for 2–3 minutes, then add the garlic and ginger. Stir-fry for 1 minute more, then add the soy sauce, sherry and salt and pepper. Stir, allow just to heat through, then pour over the spaghetti. Serve at once, without tossing.

GNOCCHI WITH TOMATO SAUCE

SERVES 4
Per serving: 360 Cals, 20 g fat, 5 g fibre

Gnocchi:
275 ml/½ pint milk
275 ml/½ pint white or vegetable stock (see pages 31–2)
1 bay leaf
100 g/4 oz wholemeal semolina
100 g/4 oz Cheddar cheese, grated
2.5 ml/½ tsp mustard powder
salt and ground black pepper
pinch nutmeg

Tomato sauce:
25 g/1 oz margarine
15 ml/1 tbsp vegetable oil
1 medium-sized onion, finely chopped
2 cloves garlic, crushed
900 g/2 lb canned tomatoes
15 ml/1 tbsp bran
1 bay leaf
5 ml/1 tsp sugar
15 ml/1 tbsp chopped parsley
5 ml/1 tsp dried oregano or basil
salt and ground black pepper

To make the gnocchi, slowly bring the milk, stock and bay leaf to the boil. Remove the bay leaf and sprinkle on the semolina, stirring. Stir over low heat for 4 minutes. Remove the pan from the heat and stir in half the cheese and the mustard. Season with salt, pepper and nutmeg and beat until the mixture is smooth. Rinse a large baking tray with cold water and turn the semolina mixture on to the tray. Smooth the top and leave to cool, then chill for 30 minutes.

Heat the oven to 190°C/375°F/Gas 5. Grease a baking dish.

Cut the gnocchi into squares and arrange in overlapping rows in the baking dish. Sprinkle the top with the reserved cheese, grind black pepper over and bake for 15–20 minutes, or until the top is golden brown. Alternatively, the gnocchi can be cooked under a moderately hot grill for 15–20 minutes, taking care not to burn the top. Serve very hot, with the tomato sauce.

To make the tomato sauce – which can be prepared well in advance and reheated – heat the margarine and oil in a pan. Fry the onion over moderate heat for 3 minutes, stirring occasionally, add the garlic and fry for 1 minute more. Tip in the tomatoes; add the bran, bay leaf, sugar and herbs; and season with salt and pepper. Bring to the boil, stirring occasionally, then simmer for about 30 minutes. Remove the bay leaf. Serve hot.

MACARONI STOVE-POT

SERVES 4
Per serving: 200 Cals, 1 g fat, 8 g fibre

1 large carrot, thinly sliced
2 small leeks, sliced
2 medium-sized potatoes, diced
275 ml/½ pint white or vegetable stock (see page 32)
175 g/6 oz short-cut wholemeal macaroni
salt
2 large tomatoes, skinned and quartered

Garnish:
15 ml/1 tbsp chopped mint

Put the vegetables into a pan with the stock, bring to the boil, cover and simmer for about 15 minutes, or until just tender. Drain.

Meanwhile, boil the macaroni in salted water for 12–13 minutes, or according to the directions on the packet, until just tender. Drain.

Stir in the macaroni and tomatoes and season with salt and pepper and allow just to heat through. Turn into a heated serving dish and sprinkle with the mint.

TOMATO AND PASTA BAKE

SERVES 4
Per serving: 200 Cals, 6 g fat, 5 g fibre

175 g/6 oz short-cut whole-meal macaroni
salt
575 ml/1 pint tomato sauce (see page 63)
30 ml/2 tbsp wholemeal breadcrumbs
40 g/1½ oz walnuts, chopped

Heat the oven to 190°C/375°F/Gas 5. Grease an ovenproof dish.

Cook the macaroni in a large pan of boiling, salted water for 12–13 minutes, or according to the directions on the packet, until just tender. Drain thoroughly and turn into the dish.

Bring the sauce just to the boil and pour over the macaroni. Bake for 25 minutes. Mix the crumbs and walnuts, scatter over the dish and continue baking for 10 minutes.

WHOLEMEAL PIZZA

SERVES 4
Per serving: 405 Cals, 16 g fat, 10 g fibre

Base:
225 g/8 oz 100% wholemeal flour
10 ml/2 tsp baking powder
pinch salt
2.5 ml/½ tsp dried mixed herbs
175 ml/6 fl oz milk

Topping:
15 ml/1 tbsp vegetable oil
2 large onions, sliced
2 cloves garlic, chopped
15 ml/1 tbsp bran
15 ml/1 tbsp chopped parsley
4 large tomatoes, sliced
2.5 ml/½ tsp sugar
2.5 ml/½ tsp dried basil
1 green pepper, sliced into rings
100 g/4 oz mushrooms, sliced
30 ml/2 tbsp stuffed green olives, sliced
salt and ground black pepper
75 g/3 oz low-fat soft cheese
75 g/3 oz Cheddar cheese, grated

Grease a baking tray. Sift together the flour, baking powder and salt, then add any bran remaining in the sieve and the herbs. Mix to a stiff dough with the milk. Roll out on a lightly floured surface and shape into a 20-cm/8-in round. Transfer to the baking tray.

Heat the oven to 220°C/425°F/Gas 7.

Heat the oil in a pan, fry the onions over moderate heat for 3 minutes, stirring occasionally, then add the garlic and fry for 1 minute more. Stir in the bran, parsley and one of the tomatoes and simmer for 2–3 minutes. Spread the onion mixture over the pizza and sprinkle with the sugar and basil. Arrange the remaining tomatoes, green pepper, mushrooms and olives in a pattern on top and season with salt and pepper. Cover with small spoonfuls of the low-fat cheese, smooth them out and then sprinkle on the grated cheese. Bake for 25–30 minutes, until the base has risen and the topping is brown and bubbling. Serve very hot.

Spaghetti with vegetable sauce (*top and centre*, see p.66), **Wholemeal pizza** (*bottom*).

64

SPAGHETTI WITH VEGETABLE SAUCE

SERVES 6
Per serving: 250 Cals, 8 g fat, 9 g fibre

400 g/14 oz wholemeal spaghetti
salt
2 medium-sized carrots, diced
1 small cauliflower, cut into flowerets
2 medium-sized courgettes, sliced
225 g/8 oz green beans, sliced
50 g/2 oz margarine
100 g/4 oz mushrooms, sliced if large
225 g/8 oz tomatoes, skinned and sliced
15 ml/1 tbsp 100% wholemeal flour
425 ml/15 fl oz white or vegetable stock (see page 32)
ground black pepper
15 ml/1 tbsp chopped oregano

Cook the spaghetti in a large pan of boiling, salted water for 12–13 minutes, or according to the directions on the packet, until just tender. Drain and keep warm.

Meanwhile, cook the carrots, cauliflower, courgettes and green beans until just tender, either in boiling, salted water or by steaming. Drain and keep warm. Melt half the margarine in a pan and fry the mushrooms and tomatoes over moderate heat for 5 minutes. Stir in the cooked vegetables.

Melt the remaining margarine in a small pan, stir in the flour and cook for 1–2 minutes. Gradually stir in the stock, bring to the boil and cook for about 3 minutes, until smooth and thickened. Stir in the oregano and pour over the vegetables, stir to mix well, then combine with the spaghetti. Toss with 2 large forks to distribute the sauce. Serve hot with, if liked, grated Parmesan cheese.

See photograph on p.65.

SPAGHETTI WITH MUSHROOM AND WALNUT SAUCE

SERVES 6
Per serving: 310 Cals, 15 g fat, 9 g fibre

400 g/14 oz wholemeal spaghetti
salt
30 ml/2 tbsp vegetable oil
1 large onion, sliced
2 cloves garlic, crushed
350 g/12 oz tomatoes, skinned and sliced
350 g/12 oz mushrooms, sliced
100 g/4 oz walnuts, roughly chopped
30 g/2 tbsp chopped parsley
ground black pepper

Garnish:
black olives

Cook the spaghetti in a large pan in plenty of boiling, salted water for about 12–13 minutes, or according to the directions on the packet, until just tender. Drain and keep warm.

Meanwhile, heat the oil in a large pan, add the onion and garlic and fry over moderate heat for 3–4 minutes. Add the sliced tomatoes and mushrooms, stir well and cover the pan. Simmer gently for about 10 minutes, shaking the pan occasionally. Add the walnuts and parsley and season with pepper. Simmer for a further 2–3 minutes. Pour the sauce over the spaghetti and toss well, using 2 forks. Serve very hot, garnished with the olives.

STOP-GO RISOTTO

SERVES 4
Per serving: 415 Cals, 17 g
fat, 4 g fibre

25 g/1 oz margarine
15 ml/1 tbsp vegetable oil
1 medium-sized onion,
  chopped
1 clove garlic, crushed
4 stalks celery, thinly sliced
225 g/8 oz brown long-grain
  rice
1 green pepper, chopped
1 red pepper, thinly sliced
100 g/4 oz mushrooms, sliced
100 g/4 oz peas, thawed
575 ml/1 pint white or
  vegetable stock (see page
  32)
salt and ground black pepper
100 g/4 oz Edam cheese,
  grated

Garnish:
15 ml/1 tbsp chopped parsley

Heat the margarine and oil in a large pan and fry the onion over moderate heat for 4 minutes, stirring occasionally. Add the garlic and celery and fry for 2 minutes. Add the rice and stir to coat the grains thoroughly with oil, then add the peppers, mushrooms and peas. Pour on the stock, season with salt and pepper and bring to the boil, stirring occasionally. Lower the heat, cover the pan and simmer without stirring for 35–40 minutes, or until the rice is tender. Add more stock if the rice dries during cooking. Stir in half the cheese and stir until it has melted.

Turn the risotto into a heated serving dish and sprinkle with the remaining cheese. Garnish with the parsley.

Alternative suggestions
A risotto is a marvellous vehicle for using small amounts of left-over cooked vegetables – cauliflower flowerets, sliced broccoli, sliced carrot and strips of fennel are especially good. Cooked meats and fish can, of course, also be added.

WHOLEMEAL CHEESE PUDDING

SERVES 4
Per serving: 400 Cals, 22 g
fat, 7 g fibre

6 slices cut from a large
  wholemeal loaf
40 g/1½ oz margarine or low-
  fat spread
10 ml/2 tsp English mustard
1 small onion, finely chopped
4 stalks celery, thinly sliced
100 g/4 oz Edam cheese,
  grated
30 ml/2 tbsp chopped parsley
5 ml/1 tsp celery seed
salt and ground black pepper
2 eggs, beaten
400 ml/14 fl oz milk

Heat the oven to 180°C/350°F/Gas 4.

Cut the crusts from the bread and spread the slices thinly with two-thirds of the margarine, then with the mustard. Cut into triangles.

Melt the remaining margarine in a small pan and fry the onion and celery over moderate heat for 3–4 minutes, stirring occasionally. Do not allow the vegetables to brown.

Cover the base of a 1.5-litre/2½-pint baking dish with some of the bread. Sprinkle some of the vegetables, cheese, parsley and celery seed over the bread and season lightly with salt and pepper. Repeat the layers of bread and flavouring, reserving about one-quarter of the cheese for the topping.

Beat together the eggs and milk and season with salt and pepper. Pour over the pudding and sprinkle with the remaining cheese. Stand the dish on a baking tray and bake for 30–35 minutes, or until the pudding is well risen and the topping crisp and golden brown. Serve hot.

LENTIL KEDGEREE

SERVES 4
Per serving: 440 Cals, 2 g fat,
12 g fibre

350 g/12 oz whole brown
lentils, soaked and drained
(see page 58)
175 g/6 oz brown long-grain
rice
10 ml/2 tsp curry powder
15 ml/1 tbsp chopped parsley
salt and ground black pepper
2 small onions, thinly sliced
into rings
1 red pepper, sliced into rings

Cook the lentils in boiling, unsalted water for 40–45 minutes, until tender. Drain thoroughly.

Meanwhile, cook the rice in boiling, salted water for 30–40 minutes, or until just tender. Drain and stir in the curry powder while still hot. Mix together the lentils and rice, stir in the parsley and season with salt and pepper. Turn into a heated serving dish and arrange the onion and pepper rings on top.

STUFFED AUBERGINES

SERVES 4
Per serving: 345 Cals, 18 g
fat, 15 g fibre

2 medium-sized aubergines
15 ml/1 tbsp vegetable oil
2 large onions, chopped
2 cloves garlic, crushed
175 g/6 oz mushrooms
4 large tomatoes, skinned and
chopped
5 ml/1 tsp tomato purée
75 g/3 oz wholemeal bread-
crumbs
30 ml/2 tbsp bran
50 g/2 oz blanched almonds,
chopped
15 ml/1 tbsp chopped parsley
5 ml/1 tsp lemon juice
salt and ground black pepper
50 g/2 oz Cheddar cheese,
grated

Heat the oven to 180°C/350°F/Gas 4.

Prick the aubergines with a fork to prevent the skins from bursting, place on a baking tray and bake for 30 minutes, turning once. Cut in halves lengthways and scoop out the flesh, leaving solid walls for the containers. Chop the flesh. Leave the oven on.

Heat the oil in a pan and fry the onions over moderate heat for 3 minutes, stirring occasionally. Add the garlic and fry for 1 minute. Chop the mushrooms and add to the pan with the tomatoes and tomato purée. Simmer for 5 minutes, stirring occasionally, then add the chopped aubergine pulp, two-thirds of the breadcrumbs, half the bran, the almonds, parsley and lemon juice and season with salt and pepper. Stir well and simmer for 2–3 minutes.

Place the aubergine shells in an ovenproof dish and spoon the filling into the shells. Mix together the remaining breadcrumbs, bran and the cheese, and sprinkle over the tops, pressing down firmly on the filling. Bake for 20–25 minutes, until the cheese is golden brown and bubbling. Serve hot.

Serving suggestions
Steamed broccoli topped with chopped walnuts or leaf spinach lightly seasoned with a pinch of nutmeg go well with a baked dish like this.

Lentil kedgeree (*above*), **Stuffed aubergines** (*below*).

LENTIL CURRY

SERVES 4
Per serving: 280 Cals, 8 g fat,
10 g fibre

225 g/8 oz whole brown lentils
1 bay leaf
2 small onions, sliced
2 cloves garlic, crushed
575 ml/1 pint white or
  vegetable stock (see pages
  31–2)
1 small cauliflower
30 ml/2 tbsp vegetable oil
4 stalks celery, thinly sliced
10 ml/2 tsp curry powder (or
  mixed curry spices, garam
  masala, if available)
2 apples, cored and sliced
15 ml/1 tbsp lemon juice
2.5 ml/½ tsp salt
15 ml/1 tbsp chopped parsley

To serve:
4 lemon wedges

Put the lentils in a pan with the bay leaf, 1 onion, 1 clove of garlic and the stock. Bring to the boil, cover and simmer gently for 40–45 minutes, stirring occasionally, or until the lentils are tender and have absorbed the stock.

Cut the cauliflower into small flowerets and steam or cook in boiling, salted water until just tender. Drain thoroughly.

Meanwhile, heat the oil in a pan and fry the remaining onion and the celery over moderate heat for 3–4 minutes. Add the remaining garlic and the curry powder or other spices and stir for 2–3 minutes. Stir in the cauliflower, apple slices, lemon juice and salt. Stir in the lentils when they are cooked and add most of the parsley. Turn into a warmed serving dish and garnish with the remaining parsley. Serve with the lemon wedges.

Serving suggestions
This curry can be served with brown rice and a selection of side dishes – such as yoghurt, chopped mint and diced cucumber; thinly sliced pepper and onion rings; tomatoes and shallots; sliced banana; desiccated coconut – and chutneys. Chappatis (see page 70), pitta bread or poppadoms make the meal more substantial.

Alternative suggestions
Other vegetables such as sliced red and green peppers, courgettes, green beans and peas can be substituted. They should retain their shape and individual characteristics, and not be stirred to a pulp.

CHAPPATIS

MAKES 12 CHAPPATIS
Per chappati: 60 Cals,
negligible fat, 2 g fibre

225 g/8 oz 100% wholemeal
  flour
pinch salt
water to mix (see method)

Mix together the flour and salt and gradually pour on just enough water to make a firm dough – the amount of water will depend on the actual flour being used. Flour your hands and divide the dough into 12 pieces. Roll each into a ball, then, on a lightly floured surface, roll each ball into a large circle. Cook each chappati on a heavy-based non-stick frying-pan or griddle for 2 minutes on each side.

Chappatis can be made in advance and reheated quickly in a frying-pan, or put on a baking tray in the oven at 180°C/350°F/Gas 4 for 10 minutes.

LENTIL CAKES

SERVES 4
Per serving: 360 Cals, 16 g fat, 15 g fibre

175 g/6 oz split red lentils
1 small onion, chopped
1 bay leaf
2.5 ml/½ tsp ground cumin
2 medium-sized tomatoes,
skinned and chopped
425 ml/15 fl oz white or
vegetable stock (see page
32)
100 g/4 oz blanched almonds,
chopped
75 g/3 oz wholemeal bread-
crumbs
30 ml/2 tbsp bran
salt and ground black pepper
30 ml/2 tbsp chopped parsley
1 egg, beaten

Put the lentils in a pan with the onion, bay leaf, cumin, tomatoes and stock. Bring to the boil, cover and simmer gently, stirring occasionally, for 30–40 minutes, or until the lentils are soft and the stock has been absorbed. Remove the bay leaf, beat the lentil purée until smooth, then leave to cool.

Heat the oven to 190°C/375°F/Gas 5. Grease a baking tray.

Mix together the almonds, breadcrumbs and bran and beat half the mixture into the lentil purée. Season with salt and pepper and stir in the parsley. Lastly, beat in the egg to bind the mixture.

Coat your hands with wholemeal flour, divide the mixture into 8 and shape them into round, flat cakes. Spread the remaining breadcrumb mixture on a plate and coat the cakes thoroughly on both sides.

Arrange the cakes on the baking tray and bake for 20–25 minutes, turning once, until golden brown. Serve hot or cold.

Serving suggestion
Lentil cakes are especially good with a spicy tomato sauce – add a pinch of cayenne or paprika pepper to the recipe on page 63. Almost any vegetable or salad can be served with them, though avoid ones noted for their dryness.

LENTIL PIE

SERVES 4
Per serving: 400 Cals, 7 g fat, 13 g fibre

350 g/12 oz split red lentils,
washed and drained
20 ml/4 tsp chopped parsley
salt and ground pepper
350 g/12 oz potatoes
15 ml/1 tbsp margarine
25 g/1 oz Edam cheese, grated

Heat the oven to 180°C/350°F/Gas 4. Grease an ovenproof dish.

Cook the lentils in boiling, unsalted water for 30–40 minutes, or until tender. Drain thoroughly and beat to a purée with a wooden spoon. Stir in half the parsley and season with salt and pepper.

Meanwhile, cook the potatoes in boiling, salted water until tender. Drain, mash with margarine and season with salt and pepper.

Spread the lentils over the base of the dish, cover with the mashed potatoes and sprinkle with the cheese. Bake for 30–35 minutes, until the top is crisp and golden brown. Sprinkle with the reserved parsley.

Fresh and Dried Beans

SERVES 4
Per serving: 190 Cals, 5 g fat, 14 g fibre

175 g/6 oz dried flageolets or haricot beans, soaked and drained
500 g/1 lb green beans, trimmed and sliced
15 ml/1 tbsp vegetable oil
10 ml/2 tsp lemon juice
salt and ground black pepper
30 ml/2 tbsp chopped summer savory or parsley

Cook the dried beans in boiling, unsalted water for about 1 hour, or until tender. Drain well and keep warm.

Meanwhile, steam the green beans or cook in boiling, salted water, until just tender. Drain.

Mix together the oil and lemon juice, season with salt and pepper and stir in most of the summer savory or parsley. Mix together the dried and green beans and, while still hot, toss in the dressing. Turn into a heated serving dish and garnish with the remaining herbs. Serve hot.

Spiced Beans

SERVES 4
Per serving: 170 Cals, 1 g fat, 16 g fibre

225 g/8 oz dried red kidney beans, soaked and drained (see page 58)
400 g/14 oz canned tomatoes
1 large onion, chopped
1 clove garlic, crushed
2.5 ml/½ tsp cayenne pepper
salt

Garnish:
15 ml/1 tbsp chopped parsley

Cook the beans in boiling, unsalted water for about 1 hour, or until nearly tender. Drain.

Boil the tomatoes, onion and garlic, cayenne pepper and a little salt for 5 minutes to reduce the liquid slightly. Add the drained beans, cover and simmer for 15 minutes. Turn into a heated serving dish and garnish with the parsley.

Serving suggestion
Spiced beans can be served as a high-fibre sauce with brown rice or as a vegetable accompaniment to flans and cold meat.

Alternative suggestion
Other dried beans can be served in the same way – haricot beans, chick peas or butter beans.

Beans Provençale

SERVES 4
Per serving: 175 Cals, 5 g fat, 16 g fibre

225 g/8 oz dried haricot beans, soaked and drained (see page 58)
400 g/14 oz canned tomatoes
1 large onion, chopped
1 clove garlic, crushed
5 ml/1 tsp dried oregano
salt and ground black pepper

Garnish:
1 small onion, sliced into rings

Cook the beans in boiling, unsalted water for about 1 hour or until tender, then drain.

Meanwhile, boil the tomatoes, onion, garlic and oregano, seasoned with salt and pepper, for 5 minutes to reduce the liquid slightly. Add the cooked, drained beans and simmer for 20 minutes. Turn into a heated serving dish and garnish with the onion rings.

Serving suggestion
A good accompaniment to a savoury flan – either as an extra vegetable or a sauce.

Beans Provençale (*above*), **Fresh and dried beans** (*below*).

BARLEY AND BEANS

SERVES 4
Per serving: 150 Cals, 2 g fat, 12 g fibre

175 g/6 oz dried black-eyed
beans – or other kidney
beans – soaked and drained
(see page 58)
40 g/1½ oz barley, soaked
and drained (see page 58)
5 ml/1 tsp vegetable oil
1 large onion, chopped·
1 clove garlic, crushed
30 ml/2 tbsp chopped parsley
salt and ground black pepper

In separate pans, cook the beans and the barley for about 1 hour, or until tender. Drain thoroughly.

Meanwhile, heat the oil in a small pan, add the onion and garlic and cook over a low heat for 10 minutes. Increase the heat and fry, stirring occasionally, until the onions turn golden brown.

Mix together the beans, barley and onion. Stir in the parsley, reserving a little for garnish. Season with salt and pepper. Turn into a heated serving dish and garnish with the reserved parsley.

Serving suggestion
Wholemeal poppadoms or chappatis (see page 70).

GARDENER'S PIE

SERVES 4
Per serving: 510 Cals, 24 g fat, 16 g fibre

Filling:
225 g/8 oz leeks, sliced
1 large onion, sliced
225 g/8 oz carrots, sliced
225 g/8 oz celery stalks, sliced
225 g/8 oz parsnips, diced
1 green pepper, sliced
25 g/1 oz margarine
25 g/1 oz 100% wholemeal
flour
275 ml/½ pint milk
75 g/3 oz cooked dried haricot
beans
salt and ground black pepper
pinch grated nutmeg

Pastry:
175 g/6 oz 100% wholemeal
flour
pinch salt
75 g/3 oz margarine
approx 30 ml/2 tbsp water
milk to glaze

Simmer the vegetables in salted water for 20 minutes, or until tender. Drain. Melt the margarine in a pan, add the flour and cook for 1 minute, stirring. Gradually pour on the milk, bring to the boil, and cook for 3 minutes, stirring. Remove from the heat. Add the haricot beans and vegetables to the sauce, season with salt, pepper and nutmeg and mix well. Turn into a 1-litre/2-pint pie dish and leave to cool.

Heat the oven to 200°C/400°F/Gas 6.

To make the pastry, mix together the flour and salt. Rub in the margarine until the mixture resembles fine breadcrumbs, add the water and mix to a firm dough. Turn on to a lightly floured surface and roll out to fit the dish. Grease the rim of the dish, press on the pastry and trim and flute the edges. Brush the pastry with milk, cut the trimmings into leaf shapes and arrange in a design. Brush with milk and pierce a hole in the centre of the pastry.

Bake for 25–30 minutes, or until golden.

Serving suggestion
Leaf spinach or a fresh green salad are good accompaniments.

BROAD BEAN SAVORY

SERVES 4
Per serving: 150 Cals, 4 g fat,
12 g fibre

10 ml/2 tsp vegetable oil
1 large onion, sliced
1 clove garlic, crushed
2 stalks celery, sliced
2 medium-sized carrots, diced
425 ml/15 fl oz white or
vegetable stock (see pages
31–2)
900 g/2 lb broad beans, shelled
15 ml/1 tbsp chopped savory
or parsley
salt and ground black pepper

Optional garnish:
15 ml/1 tbsp 'buttered' crumbs
(see page 42)

Heat the oil in a pan, add the onion and garlic and cook over a low heat for 10 minutes. Add the celery and carrots, increase heat to medium and fry, stirring occasionally, for 3 minutes. Pour in the stock, bring to the boil, cover and simmer for 15 minutes. Meanwhile, steam the beans or cook in boiling, salted water, until almost tender. Drain. Add the cooked beans and herb, season to taste with salt and pepper and simmer until all the vegetables are tender. Turn into a heated serving dish and sprinkle with the crumbs just before serving.

Serving suggestion
A dish of mixed root vegetables, such as potatoes and parsnips, or small white turnips.

SOYA BEAN CASSEROLE

SERVES 4
Per serving: 300 Cals, 12 g
fat, 5 g fibre

250 g/8 oz dried soya beans,
soaked and drained (see
page 58)
1 large onion, sliced
500 g/1 lb tomatoes, skinned
and sliced
15 ml/1 tbsp chopped parsley
15 ml/1 tbsp chopped oregano
salt and ground black pepper
275 ml/½ pint brown stock
(see page 32)
25 ml/1 oz Edam cheese,
grated

Heat the oven to 190°C/375°F/Gas 5. Grease an oven-proof dish.

Cook the soya beans in boiling, unsalted water for about 3 hours until just tender. Drain and spread half in the dish. Cover with half the onion and half the tomatoes and sprinkle with half the herbs. Season with salt and pepper. Repeat the layers, pour on the stock and sprinkle with the cheese. Cover and bake for 30 minutes. Uncover and bake for 20 minutes, until the top is crisp and brown. Serve very hot.

OVERLEAF: Ratatouille (*left,* see p.78), Red cabbage and chestnuts (*centre,* see p.78), Vegetable casserole (*right,* see p.79).

75

RED CABBAGE AND CHESTNUTS

SERVES 4

Per serving: 145 Cals, 6 g fat, 7 g fibre

1 small red cabbage, finely shredded
25 g/1 oz margarine
1 large onion, sliced
2 large cooking apples, cored and chopped
100 g/4 oz dried chestnuts, soaked, drained and coarsely chopped
30 ml/2 tbsp red wine vinegar
5 ml/1 tsp brown sugar
30 ml/2 tbsp vegetable stock (see page 32)

Heat the oven to 180°C/350°F/Gas 4. Grease an ovenproof dish.

Melt the margarine in a pan and fry the onion and apples over moderate heat for about 3 minutes, until soft but not brown. Put a layer of shredded cabbage in the bottom of the casserole, sprinkle with some of the onion and then chestnuts. Repeat the layers, finishing with cabbage. Mix together the vinegar, sugar and stock and season with salt and pepper. Pour over the cabbage, cover and cook for 1½ hours, or until the cabbage is tender.

Serving suggestion
Red cabbage is a traditional accompaniment to pork, goose and duck, but is equally good with not-so-rich dishes of lamb and beef.

See photograph on pp.76–7.

RATATOUILLE

SERVES 4

Per serving: 125 Cals, 8 g fat, 4 g fibre

1 medium-sized aubergine
salt
30 ml/2 tbsp vegetable oil
1 medium-sized onion, chopped
2 cloves garlic, crushed
1 red pepper, trimmed and sliced
1 green pepper, trimmed and sliced
225 g/8 oz courgettes, sliced
225 g/8 oz tomatoes, skinned and chopped
50-g/2-oz can tomato purée
275 ml/½ pint hot white or vegetable stock (see page 32)
ground black pepper
30 ml/2 tbsp chopped parsley

Dice the aubergine and sprinkle with salt. Leave in a colander to drain for about 30 minutes, then rinse under cold, running water. Pat dry with kitchen paper.

Heat the oil in a large pan and fry the onion and garlic over moderate heat for about 3 minutes then add the aubergine, sliced peppers, courgettes and tomatoes. Stir well, then fry for 3 minutes. Mix together the tomato purée and hot stock, season well with salt and pepper and pour over the vegetables. Bring to the boil, cover and simmer for about 30–45 minutes, until the vegetables are tender but not mushy. Stir in the parsley.

Serving suggestions
To serve hot, transfer the ratatouille to a heated dish and serve with grilled meat or fish.

To serve cold, allow to cool in the pan then chill in a covered container. Chilled ratatouille makes a good first course, or can be served to accompany flans, pasties or cold meat.

See photograph on pp.76–7.

VEGETABLE CASSEROLE

SERVES 4

Per serving: 300 Cals, 5 g fat, 10 g fibre

100 g/4 oz cooked whole lentils
500 g/1 lb potatoes, sliced
2 medium-sized carrots, sliced
1 large parsnip, thinly sliced
2 large onions, sliced
2 medium-sized leeks, sliced
100 g/4 oz sweetcorn
100 g/4 oz mushrooms, sliced
salt and ground black pepper
30 ml/2 tbsp chopped parsley
15 ml/1 tbsp chopped mint
grated rind 1 orange
850 ml/1½ pints hot white or vegetable stock (see page 32)
50 g/2 oz Cheddar cheese, grated

Heat the oven to 170°C/325°F/Gas 3.

Grease a 2-litre/3½-pint casserole and arrange all the prepared vegetables in layers, seasoning each layer with salt, pepper and herbs, finishing with a layer of overlapping slices of potato and parsnip. Mix the orange rind into the hot stock, pour over the vegetables and cover the casserole with foil, then with the lid. Stand on a baking tray and bake for 2½ hours, or until all the vegetables are tender. Remove the lid and foil, sprinkle the cheese over the top and cook under a hot grill until it bubbles and browns. Serve hot.

See photograph on pp.76–7.

HOPPIN' JOHN

SERVES 4

Per serving: 260 Cals, 1 g fat, 16 g fibre

225 g/8 oz dried black-eyed beans, soaked and drained (see page 58)
575 ml/1 pint white or vegetable stock (see page 32)
500 g/1 lb tomatoes, skinned and chopped (or canned tomatoes)
100 g/4 oz brown long-grain rice
salt and ground black pepper
pinch cayenne pepper
30 ml/2 tbsp chopped parsley

Put the beans and stock in a pan, cover, bring to the boil, then simmer for 1 hour. Add the tomatoes and rice and return to the boil. Simmer, covered, for a further 40 minutes, or until the rice is tender.

Season with salt, pepper and cayenne pepper and stir in most of the parsley. Leave the pan on the side of the stove for a few minutes to allow the flavours to blend. Turn into a heated serving dish and garnish with the reserved parsley.

Serving suggestion
A salad of crisp green leaves and chopped mint or chives is refreshing with this traditional southern American dish.

Alternative suggestion
Leaving aside authenticity, you can add small amounts of colourful cooked vegetables, or even chopped pineapple, for variety.

WHEAT AND VEGETABLE FRICASSÉE

SERVES 6
Per serving: 510 Cals, 22 g fat, 13 g fibre

225 g/8 oz whole wheat, soaked overnight
225 g/8 oz leeks, sliced
225 g/8 oz carrots, diced
225 g/8 oz cauliflower, cut into flowerets
2 stalks celery, sliced
50 g/2 oz margarine
50 g/2 oz 100% wholemeal flour
575 ml/1 pint milk
salt and ground black pepper
175 g/6 oz Cheddar cheese, grated
30 ml/2 tbsp chopped parsley
50 g/2 oz wholemeal bread-crumbs

Drain the wheat and cook in boiling, salted water for 30–35 minutes, or until soft. Drain thoroughly.

Meanwhile, steam or boil the vegetables in salted water until just tender. Drain well.

Heat the oven to 190°C/375°F/Gas 5.

Melt the margarine in a pan, stir in the flour and cook for 1 minute. Gradually stir in the milk, bring to the boil and cook for 3 minutes. Season with salt and pepper and stir in two-thirds of the cheese. Remove from the heat.

Mix the vegetables, wheat and parsley, and stir in the cheese sauce. Turn the vegetables into a shallow baking dish. Mix together the remaining cheese and the breadcrumbs and sprinkle the topping over the dish. Bake for 20–25 minutes, or until the top is golden and bubbling.

Serving suggestion
Hot, crusty bread and crunchy winter salads such as shredded cabbage and carrots, sprinkled with sunflower seeds.

AUBERGINE AND MUSHROOM FLAN

SERVES 4
Per serving: 410 Cals, 26 g fat, 7 g fibre

Pastry:
175 g/6 oz 100% wholemeal flour
pinch salt
100 g/4 oz margarine
approx 30 ml/2 tbsp water

Filling:
1 large aubergine
salt and ground black pepper
15 ml/1 tbsp chopped parsley or mint
2 eggs, beaten
100 g/4 oz low-fat cottage cheese, sieved
150 ml/5 fl oz milk
100 g/4 oz mushrooms, sliced

Aubergine and mushroom flan (*above*), **Ratatouille flan** (*below, see p.83*).

Heat the oven to 180°C/350°F/Gas 4.

To make the pastry, mix together the flour and salt, rub in the margarine until the mixture resembles fine breadcrumbs, then mix to a firm dough with the water. Wrap closely and chill for about 1 hour.

Meanwhile, prick the aubergine skin with a fork, place it on a baking tray and bake for 30 minutes, turning occasionally so that it browns evenly. (This can be done in advance when using the oven for another dish.) Cut the aubergine in half, scoop out the flesh and mash well. Season with salt and pepper and stir in the parsley or mint. Leave to cool.

Heat the oven to 200°C/400°F/Gas 6. Grease a 20-cm/8-in flan ring.

Roll out the pastry on a lightly floured surface and line the flan ring. Prick the pastry with a fork and line the base with greased foil. Fill with baking beans and bake for 12 minutes. Lower heat to 180°C/350°F/Gas 4.

Remove the lining and beans. Spread the aubergine purée over the pastry base. Beat together the eggs, cottage cheese and milk and season with salt and pepper. Pour over the aubergine and arrange the mushrooms in circles. Return the flan to the oven and bake for 30 minutes, or until set and the top golden brown. Serve warm or cold.

RED BEAN FLAN

SERVES 4
Per serving: 590 Cals, 35 g fat, 14 g fibre

Pastry:
225 g/8 oz 100% wholemeal
    flour
15 ml/1 tbsp soya flour
pinch salt
100 g/4 oz margarine
30 ml/2 tbsp water

Filling:
25 g/1 oz margarine
1 large onion, sliced
1 clove garlic, crushed
400 g/14 oz canned tomatoes
175 g/6 oz cooked, dried
    kidney or haricot beans (or
    drained canned beans)
15 ml/1 tbsp chopped oregano
ground black pepper
150 ml/5 fl oz low-fat plain
    yoghurt
1 egg

To make the pastry, sift together the flour, soya flour and salt and stir in the bran remaining in the sieve. Rub in the fat until the mixture resembles fine breadcrumbs. Stir the water into the dry ingredients to form a stiff dough. Wrap closely and chill for about 1 hour.

To make the filling, melt the margarine in a pan and fry the onion and garlic over moderate heat for about 3 minutes. Do not allow to brown. Add the tomatoes and cook, stirring occasionally, for about 20 minutes, or until the sauce has thickened. Stir in the beans and oregano and season with salt and pepper. Remove from the heat. Beat together the yoghurt and egg and beat lightly into the tomato mixture. Leave to cool.

Heat the oven to 180°C/350°F/Gas 4. Grease a 20-cm/8-in flan ring.

Roll out the pastry on a lightly floured surface and line the flan ring. Prick the pastry with a fork, cover it with greased foil and fill with baking beans. Bake for 20 minutes. Remove the beans and foil lining and pour in the bean and tomato filling. Return to the oven and bake for a further 20 minutes, or until set. Serve warm or cold.

ASPARAGUS FLAN

SERVES 4
Per serving: 475 Cals, 30 g fat, 7 g fibre

Pastry:
225 g/8 oz 100% wholemeal
    flour
pinch salt
100 g/4 oz margarine
approx 30 ml/2 tbsp water

Filling:
225 g/8 oz cooked asparagus
    (or canned asparagus,
    drained)
2 eggs
275 ml/½ pint milk
15 ml/1 tbsp chopped parsley
salt and ground black pepper
50 g/2 oz mushrooms, thinly
    sliced, or 1 green pepper,
    thinly sliced into rings

To make the pastry, sift together the flour and salt, mix in the bran remaining in the sieve and rub in the margarine until the mixture resembles fine bread-crumbs. Mix to a firm dough with the water. Wrap closely and chill for about 1 hour.

Heat the oven to 190°C/375°F/Gas 5 and grease a 20-cm/8-in flan ring.

Roll out the pastry on a lightly floured surface and line the greased flan ring. Prick the pastry with a fork, line the base with foil and fill with baking beans. Bake for 10 minutes. Remove the beans and lining and bake for 5 minutes to dry the pastry base.

Chop the asparagus and arrange in the flan case. Beat together the eggs and milk, stir in the parsley and season with salt and pepper. Pour over the asparagus and arrange the mushrooms or pepper in a pattern. Bake for 30–35 minutes, or until set. Serve warm or cold.

RATATOUILLE FLAN

SERVES 4
Per serving: 510 Cals, 32 g
fat, 10 g fibre

Pastry:
*75 g/3 oz 81% wheatmeal
self-raising flour (see page
108)*
150 g/5 oz coarse oatmeal
pinch salt
100 g/4 oz margarine
approx 60 ml/4 tbsp water

Filling:
30 ml/2 tbsp vegetable oil
1 large onion, sliced
1 red pepper, sliced
1 green pepper, sliced
500 g/1 lb courgettes, sliced
500 g/1 lb tomatoes, sliced
2 cloves garlic, crushed
salt and ground black pepper
15 ml/1 tbsp chopped parsley

Heat the oven to 190°C/375°F/Gas 5. Grease a 23-cm/9-in flan ring.

To make the pastry, mix together the flour, oatmeal and salt and rub in the margarine. Mix to a firm but not sticky dough with the water. Roll out on a lightly floured surface and line the flan ring. Prick the pastry with a fork, line with greased foil and fill with baking beans. Bake for 25 minutes. Remove the foil and beans and return to the oven for 5 minutes to dry the pastry base.

To make the filling, heat the oil in a medium-sized pan, add the onion and fry over moderate heat for 5 minutes, stirring occasionally. Add the peppers and courgettes, cook for a further 10 minutes, then add the tomatoes and garlic. Season with salt and pepper and continue cooking for a further 20 minutes, until the vegetables are tender and the mixture has thickened. Stir in the parsley and adjust seasoning if necessary.

Spoon into the pastry case. To serve hot, return the flan to the oven for 5–10 minutes, then serve at once. To serve cold, first reheat pastry and filling together, then allow to cool.

Serving suggestion
No other vegetables or salad are necessary with this main course. Wholemeal French bread, if available, or hot wholemeal rolls and garlic butter are ideal accompaniments.

Garlic 'butter' beat 100 g/4 oz unsalted butter or low-fat spread until light. Beat in 2 crushed cloves garlic, 10 ml/2 tsp chopped parsley and a few drops of lemon juice, and season to taste with salt and pepper. To store, close-wrap in foil and keep in the refrigerator, or freeze.

See photograph on p.80.

5 FISH, POULTRY AND MEAT

It may well be that the ever-rising price of meat and the threatened world protein shortage will eventually have a beneficial effect on our general health, persuading us, as medical evidence has so far failed to do, to eat less of this high-protein but high-fat food.

There is no need, unless we wish, to go to the length of adopting a strict vegetarian programme, but we should at least learn to use meat in smaller quantities, combining it with larger amounts of vegetables, especially pulses, wholemeal pasta, brown rice and wholemeal flour.

Meat contains the saturated fats, which are thought to be a contributing factor in the incidence of heart disease. Saturated fats are generally those which set solid when cold.

Switching to unsaturated fats – in the form of white fish, soft margarine, low-fat spread, sunflower oil and corn oil – can help to reduce the risk of heart disease.

Goose, duck, bacon, pork and (even lean) beef and lamb have the highest fat content. Chicken and turkey – without the skin, which is high in fat – and white fish have the lowest fat content. That is why poultry and white fish feature strongly in the following recipes.

By removing the 'visible' fat on meat you won't, in fact, be removing all the fat as there is 'invisible' fat actually within the meat.

When cooking meat, get used to dry-frying off the fat in a non-stick pan and then *discarding it* before adding other ingredients.

A white sauce can be made without fat by gradually blending together the wholemeal flour and milk or skimmed milk, then heating gently in a small pan, stirring all the time until it boils and thickens. It will not taste the same, but it produces a sauce that complements vegetables and whole grains particularly well.

Add bran or wholemeal semolina to casseroled dishes to add fibre and to thicken.

Fish and sweetcorn casserole (*above*, **see p.87**), **Fish kebabs with sweetcorn** (*below*, **see p.87**).

FISH

BAKED FINNAN POTATOES

SERVES 4
Per serving: 280 Cals, 9 g fat, 3 g fibre

4 large potatoes, scrubbed
225 g/8 oz cooked smoked haddock fillets, skinned and flaked
25 g/1 oz margarine
30 ml/2 tbsp low-fat plain yoghurt
15 ml/1 tbsp whole-grain mustard
salt and ground black pepper
2 rashers bacon, rinds removed

Heat oven to 190°C/350°F/Gas 5.

Dry the potatoes, prick with a fork to prevent them bursting, and bake for 1–1¼ hours, until tender.

Meanwhile, cut the bacon into small dice and fry until the fat runs. Remove with a slotted spoon, discarding the fat.

Cut the cooked potatoes in half and scoop the flesh into a bowl. Stir in the fish, margarine, yoghurt and mustard and season well with salt and pepper. Pile into the potato shells, place on a baking tray and sprinkle the bacon over. Return to the oven for 10–15 minutes.

Serve hot. Be sure to encourage everyone to eat the potato skins, which are not only high in fibre, they're delicious!

Serving suggestion
A crisp salad of finely shredded hard white cabbage and nuts.

KEDGEREE

SERVES 4
Per serving: 270 Cals, 7 g fat, 2 g fibre

500 g/1 lb cooked smoked haddock fillets
25 g/1 oz margarine
1 large onion, finely chopped
10 ml/2 tsp curry powder
175 g/6 oz brown long-grain rice
5 ml/1 tsp lemon juice
75 g/3 oz sultanas
575 ml/1 pint white stock (see page 31), or water
salt and ground black pepper
2 bay leaves
30 ml/2 tbsp chopped parsley

Garnish:
1 lemon, quartered

Place the fish in a frying-pan or shallow dish and cover with boiling water. Leave for 3 minutes, then drain. Remove the skin and any bones from the fish and flake it.

Melt the margarine in the rinsed frying-pan and fry the onion over moderate heat for about 3 minutes, stirring occasionally. Stir in the curry powder, cook for 2 minutes then stir in the rice, lemon juice and sultanas. Gradually pour on the stock or water, bring to the boil and season with salt and pepper. Add the bay leaf, cover and simmer very gently, without stirring, for about 40 minutes. Stir in the fish, cover and continue cooking for 10 minutes until the liquid has been absorbed and the rice is tender. Remove the bay leaves. Stir in the parsley, turn into a heated serving dish and garnish with the lemon wedges.

Serving suggestion
A salad of sliced green peppers, diced cucumber and onion rings in a yoghurt dressing very lightly flavoured with a dash of mango sauce.

FISH KEBABS WITH SWEETCORN

SERVES 4
Per serving: 450 Cals, 9 g fat,
5 g fibre

45 ml/3 tbsp clear honey
30 ml/2 tbsp lemon juice
15 ml/1 tbsp soy sauce
large pinch cayenne pepper
8 small whiting fillets, skinned
12 small pickling onions
4 courgettes
8 small bay leaves
175 g/6 oz brown long-grain
rice
4 × corn on the cob, trimmed
25 g/1 oz margarine, melted
salt and ground black pepper

See photograph on p.85.

Put the honey, lemon juice, soy sauce and cayenne pepper in a small pan and heat until the honey melts. Pour into a shallow dish and leave to cool.

Cut the fish into large chunks. Skin the onions and blanch in boiling water for 2–3 minutes, then drain thoroughly. Slice the courgettes into 2.5-cm/1-in slices.

Divide the fish, onions, courgettes and bay leaves into 4 portions and thread alternately on to 4 skewers and lay in the sauce in the dish. Turn frequently and leave for at least 1 hour – or overnight, if more convenient.

Cook the rice in plenty of boiling, salted water for 30–40 minutes until just tender. Drain and turn on to a heated serving dish.

Meanwhile, brush the sweetcorn with the melted margarine and season the kebabs and sweetcorn with salt and pepper. Grill under moderate-to-high heat for 15 minutes, turning both skewers and sweetcorn frequently and brushing the kebabs with the remaining basting sauce.

Arrange the kebabs and sweetcorn on top of the rice, and pour over any remaining marinade.

FISH AND SWEETCORN CASSEROLE

SERVES 4
Per serving: 410 Cals, 10 g
fat, 11 g fibre

25 g/1 oz margarine
2 large onions, sliced
1 clove garlic, crushed
350 g/12 oz canned tomatoes
350 g/12 oz canned sweetcorn,
drained
1 green pepper, trimmed and
sliced
700 g/1½ lb white fish fillet
(e.g. cod, whiting, haddock),
skinned
15 ml/1 tbsp made mustard
salt and ground black pepper
50 g/2 oz wholemeal breadcrumbs
25 g/1 oz Bran Flakes
25 g/1 oz Cheddar cheese,
grated

Heat the oven to 190°C/375°F/Gas 5.

Melt the margarine in an ovenproof casserole and fry the onions over moderate heat for about 3 minutes, until soft but not brown. Add the garlic, tomatoes, sweetcorn, green pepper and mustard. Stir and bring to the boil.

Cut the fish into 5-cm/2-in pieces. Add to the casserole, season with salt and pepper, cover and cook in the oven for 20–25 minutes, until the sauce has thickened and the fish is firm.

Mix together the breadcrumbs, Bran Flakes and cheese and sprinkle on the casserole. Return to the oven for 10 minutes, or until the topping is crisp and golden brown.

Serving suggestions
Small potatoes boiled in their jackets and a crisp, green salad of sliced raw leeks or onions, watercress or crisp lettuce and chopped celery leaves.

See photograph on p.85.

FISH CREOLE

SERVES 4
Per serving: 300 Cals, 12 g
fat, 4 g fibre

*1 large green pepper, trimmed
and sliced
1 large red pepper, trimmed
and sliced
1 large onion, sliced
5 ml/1 tsp dried basil
400 g/14 oz canned tomatoes
2.5 ml/½ tsp Tabasco sauce
salt and ground black pepper
500 g/1 lb white fish fillet (e.g.
cod, whiting, haddock),
skinned*

Topping:
*50 g/2 oz rolled oats
50 g/2 oz 100% wholemeal
flour
salt and ground black pepper
25 g/1 oz margarine
50 g/2 oz Cheddar cheese,
grated*

Simmer the peppers, onion, basil, tomatoes and Tabasco in a small pan for 20 minutes until the sauce has thickened. Season with salt and pepper.

Cut the fish into large pieces, arrange in a greased baking dish and pour the sauce over.

Heat the oven to 200°C/400°F/Gas 6.

To make the topping, stir together the oats, flour and salt, season with pepper and rub in the fat. Stir in the cheese and sprinkle over the fish. Bake for 20–25 minutes, or until the topping is crisp and golden brown.

Serving suggestions
A crisp green salad of lettuce, chicory and chives with a lemon dressing, or thinly sliced raw Brussels sprouts and leeks with watercress or Chinese leaves.

BELOW: Fish Creole (*left*),
Norfolk fish pie (*right*).

NORFOLK FISH PIE

SERVES 4
Per serving: 350 Cals, 4 g fat, 10 g fibre

225 g/8 oz carrots, sliced
225 g/8 oz leeks, sliced
1 celery heart, sliced
salt
500 g/1 lb potatoes, sliced
700 g/1½ lb white fish fillet
425 ml/15 fl oz milk and water
60 ml/4 tbsp low-fat plain yoghurt
25 g/1 oz margarine
25 g/1 oz 100% wholemeal flour
10 ml/2 tsp mustard powder
ground black pepper
pinch ground mace
500 g/1 lb tomatoes, thinly sliced
45 ml/3 tbsp Bran Flakes

Cook the vegetables until tender.

Meanwhile, simmer the fish, milk and water for 10 minutes. Strain and reserve the liquid. Skin the fish and remove any bones. Cut into large chunks.

Heat the oven to 200°C/400°F/Gas 6.

Melt the margarine in a pan, stir in the flour and cook over moderate heat for 1 minute. Gradually stir in the reserved stock, and cook until the sauce thickens. Mix the mustard powder to a smooth paste with a little cold water and stir into the sauce. Season well with salt, pepper and mace. Drain the vegetables. Mash the potatoes with the yoghurt and stir the other vegetables into the sauce with the fish. Turn mixture into a 1-litre/2-pint baking dish and cover with the tomatoes. Spread the mashed potato over the dish to cover the tomatoes completely. Bake for 15 minutes, sprinkle on the Bran Flakes and return to the oven for 5 minutes. Garnish with parsley and serve very hot.

Garnish:
parsley sprigs

FISHCAKES WITH ONION SAUCE

SERVES 4

Per serving: 225 Cals, 9 g fat, 5 g fibre

225 g/8 oz cooked, boneless white fish (e.g. cod, whiting, haddock), skinned and flaked
225 g/8 oz mashed potato
25 g/1 oz margarine, melted
30 ml/2 tbsp bran
10 ml/2 tsp made mustard
15 ml/1 tbsp chopped parsley
salt and ground black pepper
50 g/2 oz dried wholemeal breadcrumbs

Onion sauce:
25 g/1 oz margarine
2 medium-sized onions, finely chopped
15 g/½ oz 100% wholemeal flour
15 ml/1 tbsp made mustard
5 ml/1 tsp cider vinegar
225 ml/8 fl oz milk
salt and ground black pepper

Garnish:
parsley sprigs

Heat the oven to 190°C/375°F/Gas 5. Grease a baking tray.

Mix together the fish, potato, margarine, bran, mustard and parsley and season with salt and pepper. Cover and chill for 10 minutes to make the mixture easier to handle. Shape into 8 small, flat cakes and turn in the breadcrumbs to coat thoroughly. Arrange on the baking tray and bake for 10 minutes, turning once, until piping hot and golden brown.

To make the sauce, melt the margarine in a pan and fry the onions over moderate heat for about 10 minutes, stirring often. Do not allow to brown. Add the flour, stir for 1 minute, then stir in the mustard and vinegar. Gradually stir in the milk and bring to the boil. Season with salt and pepper and boil gently for 3 minutes.

Transfer the fish cakes to a heated dish and garnish with the parsley. Serve the onion sauce separately.

Serving suggestions
A mixture of vegetables such as peas, carrots and sweetcorn to add colour and texture to the dish; or broccoli spears topped with a few dill or fennel seeds; or green beans and grilled tomatoes.

SPICED FISH SOUFFLÉ

SERVES 4

Per serving: 210 Cals, 11 g fat, 2 g fibre

25 g/1 oz margarine
100 g/4 oz mashed potato
25 g/1 oz Cheddar cheese, grated
45 ml/3 tbsp milk
30 ml/2 tbsp bran
salt and ground black pepper
5 ml/1 tsp curry powder
225 g/8 oz cooked smoked haddock fillet, skinned and flaked
egg yolk
3 egg whites

Heat the oven to 200°C/400°F/Gas 6. Grease a 15-cm/6-in soufflé dish.

Melt the margarine in a pan, beat in the mashed potato, cheese, milk and bran and season with salt, pepper and the curry powder. Remove the pan from the heat and beat in the fish and egg yolk. Allow to cool. Whisk the egg whites until stiff, then fold them into the fish mixture. Spoon into the soufflé dish and bake for 30–35 minutes, until the soufflé is well risen and golden brown on top. Serve at once.

Serving suggestion
A crisp, crunchy salad with a tangy, lemon dressing – chicory, celery and lettuce garnished with fresh orange segments or apple slices, for example.

FISH RATATOUILLE

SERVES 4
Per serving: 290 Cals, 16 g fat, 6 g fibre

40 g/1½ oz margarine, melted
4 × 175 g/6 oz white fish fillets, skinned
salt and ground black pepper
1 medium-sized onion, chopped
100 g/4 oz mushrooms, sliced
1 green pepper, trimmed and sliced
4 tomatoes, peeled and sliced
2 small courgettes, sliced
2.5 ml/½ tsp dried oregano
50 g/2 oz Cheddar cheese, grated
45 ml/3 tbsp Bran Flakes

Brush a little margarine over both sides of the fish, season with salt and pepper and roll up, skinned sides out. Grill under moderate heat for about 5 minutes, turning to cook them evenly.

Heat the oven to 200°C/400°F/Gas 6. Grease a shallow baking dish.

Fry the onion in the remaining margarine over moderate heat for about 3 minutes, then add the mushrooms, tomatoes, courgettes and oregano, and season well with salt and pepper. Cook for 5 minutes. Turn into the dish and arrange the fish on top. Mix together the cheese and Bran Flakes, sprinkle over the dish, taking care to cover the fish completely. Bake for 15–20 minutes, until the top is golden brown.

Serving suggestion
With a one-pot meal like this, a basket of hot, crusty wholemeal bread rolls will probably be enough.

FISH COBBLER

SERVES 4
Per serving: 330 Cals, 12 g fat, 7 g fibre

15 ml/1 tbsp vegetable oil
1 large onion, thinly sliced
2 medium-sized carrots, diced
2 stalks celery, thinly sliced
100 g/4 oz button mushrooms, sliced
225 g/8 oz tomatoes, peeled and sliced
salt and ground black pepper
15 ml/1 tbsp lemon juice
700 g/1½ lb white fish fillet (e.g. cod, whiting, haddock), skinned

Topping:
4 slices wholemeal bread lightly spread with margarine or low-fat spread

Heat the oven to 200°C/400°F/Gas 6.

Heat the oil in an ovenproof casserole and fry the onion over moderate heat for about 3 minutes. Add the carrots and celery, stir and cook for 2 minutes. Add the mushrooms and tomatoes, season with salt and pepper and stir in the lemon juice. Cut the fish into large chunks and carefully stir into the casserole.

Cut the bread into triangles and arrange over the casserole 'buttered' side up. Bake for 15–20 minutes, until the topping is crisp.

Serving suggestion
A green vegetable such as broccoli or spinach.

POULTRY AND MEAT

CHICKEN AND BEANSPROUTS

SERVES 4

Per serving: 240 Cals; 13 g fat, 4 g fibre

2 × 350 g/12 oz chicken portions, skinned
30 ml/2 tbsp vegetable oil
1 medium-sized onion, thinly sliced
1 clove garlic, crushed
30 ml/2 tbsp soy sauce
2.5 ml/½ tsp ground ginger
5 ml/1 tsp brown sugar
salt
500 g/1 lb fresh beansprouts

Cut the chicken from the bones and cut into thin strips. Heat the oil in a pan and fry the onion and garlic over moderate heat for 1 minute. Add the chicken, soy sauce, ginger, sugar and salt and stir-fry for 3 minutes. Add the beansprouts, stir well and fry for a further 2 minutes, stirring. Do not allow the beansprouts to overcook and become soft. Transfer to a heated serving dish and serve at once.

Serving suggestion
Brown rice with peas and sweetcorn and a green vegetable such as spinach or sliced green beans.

CHICKEN GOULASH

SERVES 4

Per serving: 533 Cals, 10 g fat, 7 g fibre

4 chicken breasts, skinned
salt and ground black pepper
30 ml/2 tbsp paprika pepper
15 ml/1 tbsp vegetable oil
2 medium-sized onions, finely chopped
4 stalks celery, sliced
1 large leek, sliced
1 green pepper, trimmed and chopped
1 red pepper, trimmed and chopped
100 g/4 oz mushrooms, sliced
50 g/2 oz tomato purée
30 ml/2 tbsp bran
45 ml/3 tbsp white stock (see page 31)
275 ml/10 fl oz low-fat plain yoghurt
275 g/10 oz wholemeal noodles

Garnish:
sprigs of mint (optional)

Toss the chicken breasts in salt, pepper and paprika to coat them. Heat the oil in a pan and fry the chicken over moderate heat for 8–10 minutes, until evenly brown. Remove from the pan. Add vegetables and any remaining paprika, stir well, cover the pan and cook over very low heat for 5 minutes. Stir in the tomato purée and cook for 1 minute. Stir in the bran and stock and return the chicken to the pan. Cover and cook over low heat, stirring frequently, for 30 minutes, or until the chicken is tender. Add a little more stock if the sauce becomes too dry. Taste and adjust seasoning if necessary. Stir in most of the yoghurt. Allow just to heat through, then turn into a heated serving dish.

Meanwhile, cook the noodles in plenty of boiling, salted water for 12–13 minutes, or according to the directions on the packet, until just tender. Drain thoroughly and arrange around the goulash. Pour over the remaining yoghurt to serve. Garnish with the mint, if wanted.

Serving suggestion
A salad of chilled, pale green leaves makes a good contrast – such as sliced Chinese cabbage, endive and cucumber garnished with plenty of chopped mint.

Chicken goulash (*above*),
Chicken and bean paella (*below*, see p.94).

CHICKEN AND BEAN PAELLA

SERVES 4

Per serving: 435 Cals, 9 g fat, 10 g fibre

425 ml/15 fl oz water
225 g/8 oz brown long-grain rice
2.5 ml/½ tsp ground turmeric
1 medium-sized aubergine
2 × 275 g/10 oz chicken joints, skinned
15 ml/1 tbsp vegetable oil
1 large onion, finely chopped
1 clove garlic, finely chopped
1 stalk celery, chopped
1 green pepper, trimmed and chopped
2 large tomatoes, skinned and chopped
100 g/4 oz mushrooms, sliced
100 g/4 oz cooked kidney beans
salt and ground black pepper
30 ml/2 tbsp chopped parsley

Bring the water to the boil in a large pan, add the rice, salt and turmeric and stir well to prevent the rice from sticking. Cover and simmer for 30 minutes without stirring. Remove from the heat.

Meanwhile, dice the aubergine and sprinkle with salt. Leave in a colander to drain for 30 minutes then rinse thoroughly under cold, running water. Pat dry with absorbent kitchen paper.

Meanwhile, cut the chicken from the bone and cut the flesh into dice. Heat the oil in a frying-pan and fry the onion, garlic, celery, pepper and aubergine over a moderate heat for 3 minutes. Do not allow to brown.

Add the chicken to the pan and cook for 5 minutes, stirring occasionally. Add the tomatoes and mushrooms, stir well and cook for 3–4 minutes. Stir in the beans and chicken-and-vegetable mixture into the rice, cover and cook over low heat for 10 minutes. Remove from the heat and leave for 5 minutes. Season with salt and pepper and stir in the parsley. Transfer to a heated serving dish.

See photograph on p.93.

CHICKEN RISOTTO

SERVES 4

Per serving: 400 Cals, 5 g fat, 4 g fibre

5 ml/1 tsp vegetable oil
1 large onion, finely chopped
2 cloves garlic, crushed
1 green pepper, trimmed and thinly sliced
225 g/8 oz brown long-grain rice
150 ml/5 fl oz dry white wine or dry cider
100 g/4 oz seedless raisins
850 ml/1½ pints white stock (see page 31)
salt and ground black pepper
225 g/8 oz cooked chicken, thinly sliced
45 ml/3 tbsp chopped parsley
a little grated Edam cheese (optional)

Heat the oil in a frying-pan and cook the onion and garlic over low heat for about 10 minutes, stirring occasionally. Do not allow to brown. Add the sliced pepper and rice and stir for 1 minute. Pour in the wine or cider, increase the heat and boil until the liquid has reduced by about a half. Add the raisins and stock, season with salt and pepper and stir well. Cover and simmer gently for about 40 minutes, or until the liquid has been absorbed and the rice is tender. Add the chicken and cook for 5 minutes. Stir in the parsley, transfer to a heated serving dish and sprinkle with a little grated Edam cheese, if liked.

Serving suggestion
Green salad and wholemeal bread.

Alternative suggestions
Cooked lamb, turkey, veal or rabbit can be used in place of the chicken.

CHICKEN CURRY

SERVES 4

Per serving: 670 Cals, 26 g fat, 9 g fibre

4 × 350 g/12 oz chicken pieces, skinned
10 ml/2 tsp salt
30 ml/2 tbsp vegetable oil
2 large onions, finely chopped
2 cloves garlic, crushed
4 stalks celery, thinly sliced
15 ml/1 tbsp finely chopped, peeled dried ginger root
5 ml/1 tsp ground cumin
5 ml/1 tsp ground turmeric
5 ml/1 tsp ground coriander
2.5 ml/½ tsp ground fennel
90 ml/6 tbsp white stock (see page 31)
225 g/8 oz tomatoes, skinned and chopped
90 ml/6 tbsp low-fat plain yoghurt
5 ml/1 tsp garam masala (mixed spice powder)
4 apples, cored and sliced
juice 1 lemon
50 g/2 oz desiccated coconut
175 g/6 oz brown long-grain rice

Dry the chicken with kitchen paper and sprinkle with salt. Heat the oil in a pan and fry the chicken over moderately high heat for 5–6 minutes, turning the pieces to brown them evenly. The flesh should be white and firm. Remove and keep warm.

Add the onions, garlic, celery and ginger to the pan and fry over moderate heat for a few minutes, stirring, until the onions are golden brown, taking care not to let them burn. Reduce the heat to low, stir in the spices and 15 ml/1 tbsp stock and stir for 1 minute. Stir in the tomatoes, yoghurt and remaining stock. Return the chicken to the pan and bring to the boil. Sprinkle the *garam masala* over the top, cover and simmer for 15 minutes. Add the sliced apples, cover, and cook for 5 minutes.

Arrange the chicken on a heated serving dish, pour the sauce over and sprinkle with lemon juice, then with the coconut.

Meanwhile, cook the rice in a large pan of boiling, salted water for about 30–40 minutes, or until just tender. Drain thoroughly and arrange in a ring round the curry.

Serving suggestions
The traditional side dishes add extra fibre – cool diced, unpeeled cucumber and chopped mint leaves stirred into chilled, low-fat plain yoghurt; wholemeal pitta bread (or naan) and poppadoms; salads of sliced raw onions, red and green peppers; oranges and bananas.

SPAGHETTI WITH BROCCOLI AND CHICKEN SAUCE

SERVES 4–6

Per serving for 4: 420 Cals, 7 g fat, 13 g fibre

400 g/14 oz wholemeal spaghetti
salt
500 g/1 lb broccoli spears
175 g/6 oz cooked chicken, thinly sliced
150 ml/5 fl oz low-fat plain yoghurt
ground black pepper
1 clove garlic, crushed
15 ml/1 tbsp chopped stoned dates
15 ml/1 tbsp chopped walnuts

Cook the spaghetti in a large pan of boiling, salted water for 12–13 minutes, or according to the directions on the packet, until just tender. Drain and keep hot.

Meanwhile, steam the broccoli or boil in salted water, until just tender. Drain thoroughly.

Heat the chicken gently with the yoghurt, pepper and garlic until just simmering. Season with salt, pour over the broccoli and stir in the dates.

Turn the spaghetti into a heated serving dish, pour the sauce over, toss well and sprinkle with the nuts.

Serving suggestion
A salad of Chinese leaves and tomatoes, or grated cabbage and celery.

CHINESE ONE-POT

SERVES 4

Per serving: 260 Cals, 13 g fat, 4 g fibre

2 × 350 g/12 oz chicken pieces, skinned
5 ml/1 tsp cornflour
15 ml/1 tbsp dry vermouth
15 ml/1 tbsp soy sauce
salt
15 ml/1 tbsp vegetable oil
1 clove garlic, crushed
2 spring onions, sliced
2 medium-sized carrots, diced
225 g/8 oz broccoli, in small flowerets
150 ml/5 fl oz white stock (see page 31)
2 stalks celery, thinly sliced
50 g/2 oz mushrooms, sliced

Cut the chicken from the bones, slice it thinly and mix with the cornflour, vermouth and soy sauce and season with salt.

Heat the oil in a large pan, add the garlic and spring onions and fry over moderate heat stirring, for 1 minute. Add the chicken, stir and fry for 3 minutes, then add the carrots and broccoli. Stir-fry for a further 2 minutes. Pour on the stock, add the celery and mushrooms and cover the pan. Bring to the boil, then simmer for about 3 minutes, or until the vegetables are barely tender – they should remain crunchy.

Turn into a heated serving dish and sprinkle with the walnuts.

Serving suggestion
Brown rice or wholemeal noodles.

Garnish:
25 g/1 oz walnuts, chopped

CHICKEN CASSEROLE WITH SURPRISE DUMPLINGS

SERVES 4

Per serving: 635 Cals, 30 g fat, 8 g fibre

4 × 275 g/10 oz chicken joints
30 ml/2 tbsp 100% wholemeal flour
salt and ground black pepper
5 ml/1 tsp mixed dried herbs
25 g/1 oz margarine
15 ml/1 tbsp vegetable oil
1 large onion, finely chopped
1 clove garlic, crushed
400 g/14 oz canned tomatoes
175 g/6 oz canned sweetcorn
500 ml/18 fl oz cider

Dumplings:
75 g/3 oz 100% wholemeal flour
large pinch salt
10 ml/2 tsp baking powder
40 g/1½ oz margarine
5 ml/1 tsp dried oregano
approx 45 ml/3 tbsp milk
8 stuffed green olives

Heat the oven to 180°C/350°F/Gas 4.

Cut each chicken joint in half. Season the flour with salt, pepper and mixed herbs and toss the chicken pieces to coat thoroughly. Melt the margarine and oil in a pan and fry the chicken over moderate heat until golden brown all over. Transfer to a casserole and keep warm. Fry the onion and garlic in the fat remaining in the pan for 3–4 minutes, then add the tomatoes, sweetcorn and cider, stir well and bring to the boil. Pour over the chicken, cover and cook for 30–40 minutes.

Meanwhile, make the dumplings. Sift the flour, salt and baking powder into a bowl and add the bran remaining in the sieve. Rub in the margarine until the mixture resembles fine breadcrumbs. Add the oregano and just enough milk to mix to a firm dough. Divide into 8 and shape each piece round an olive. Place on top of the casserole and continue cooking, uncovered, for 20 minutes.

Serving suggestion
Brown rice tossed with peas and garnished with a little grated cheese.

Chicken casserole with surprise dumplings.

96

SPICED CHICKEN WITH PASTA

SERVES 4

Per serving: 590 Cals, 19 g fat, 4 g fibre

15 ml/1 tbsp vegetable oil
1 large onion, thinly sliced
1 clove garlic, crushed
4 stalks celery, thinly sliced
5–10 ml/1–2 tsp curry powder
5 ml/1 tsp ground coriander
pinch cayenne pepper
pinch ground ginger
425 ml/15 fl oz white stock
   (see page 31)
500 g/1 lb cooked chicken,
   diced
30 ml/2 tbsp mango or peach
   chutney, chopped
25 g/1 oz sultanas
salt and ground black pepper
150 ml/5 fl oz low-fat plain
   yoghurt
225 g/8 oz wholemeal pasta
   shapes

Heat the oil in a pan and fry the onion over moderate heat for 3 minutes, add the garlic and celery and fry, stirring occasionally, for 3 minutes. Stir in the spices and cook for 1 minute, then gradually pour on the stock. Bring to the boil, cover and simmer for 15 minutes. Add the chicken, chutney and sultanas and continue cooking for 5 minutes. Season with salt and pepper, stir in the yoghurt and allow just to heat through.

Meanwhile, cook the pasta in plenty of boiling, salted water for 12–13 minutes, or according to the directions on the packet, until just tender. Drain and turn into a heated serving dish. Pour the chicken sauce over and garnish with the walnuts.

Serving suggestion
A salad of red and green peppers and onions sliced into rings, or sliced banana tossed in lemon juice, to preserve the colour, and mixed with raisins or finely chopped dried apricots.

Garnish:
40 g/1½ oz walnuts, chopped

GREEN SPAGHETTI CHICKEN

SERVES 4

Per serving: 380 Cals, 8 g fat, 9 g fibre

350 g/12 oz wholemeal
   spaghetti
salt
15 ml/1 tbsp vegetable oil
1 medium-sized onion, finely
   chopped
2 medium-sized courgettes,
   thinly sliced
225 g/ 8 oz cooked chicken,
   diced
15 ml/1 tbsp chopped tarragon
60 ml/4 tbsp dry white wine
   or dry cider
ground black pepper

Garnish:
30 ml/2 tbsp chopped parsley

Cook the spaghetti in a large pan of boiling, salted water for 12–13 minutes, or according to the directions on the packet, until just tender.

Meanwhile, heat the oil in a pan and fry the onion and courgettes over moderate heat, stirring occasionally, for 5 minutes. Add the chicken, tarragon and wine or cider and cook quickly until the liquid has evaporated.

When the spaghetti is cooked, drain thoroughly and return to the rinsed pan. Add the chicken and vegetable mixture, season with salt and pepper and toss well. Turn at once into a heated serving dish and garnish with the parsley.

Alternative suggestions
This is also a good way of stretching a little left-over turkey or white fish.

GOLDEN CHICKEN PASTA

SERVES 4
Per serving: 430 Cals, 12 g fat, 7 g fibre

25 g/1 oz margarine
1 large onion, chopped
15 ml/1 tbsp curry powder
2.5 ml/½ tsp ground ginger
40 g/1½ oz 100% wholemeal flour
575 ml/1 pint white stock (see page 31)
30 ml/2 tbsp mango chutney
350 g/12 oz cooked chicken, diced
225 g/8 oz wholemeal pasta shapes
30 ml/2 tbsp sultanas
150 ml/5 fl oz low-fat plain yoghurt

Melt the margarine in a pan and fry the onion over moderate heat for 3–4 minutes. Stir in the curry powder and ginger, fry for 1 minute, then stir in the flour, and fry for 1 minute. Pour on the stock and bring to the boil, still stirring. Add the chutney and chicken, cover and simmer for 20 minutes.

Meanwhile, cook the pasta in plenty of boiling, salted water for 12–13 minutes, or according to the directions on the packet, until just tender. Drain and turn into a greased serving dish. Add the sultanas and yoghurt to the pan, stir well and allow just to heat through. Pour over the pasta and toss to blend thoroughly.

Serving suggestion
This lightly spiced chicken and pasta dish takes well to traditional curry accompaniments – sliced banana (tossed in lemon juice to preserve the colour), shredded coconut, green pepper and onion rings, and yoghurt-and-cucumber salad.

TURKEY EN CROUTE

SERVES 4
Per serving: 535 Cals, 32 g fat, 7 g fibre

Pastry:
225 g/8 oz 100% wholemeal flour
pinch salt
100 g/4 oz margarine
approx 60 ml/4 tbsp water

Filling:
400 g/14 oz turkey pieces (boned weight)
15 ml/1 tbsp vegetable oil
1 small onion, finely chopped
100 g/4 oz low-fat soft cheese
100 g/4 oz canned sweetcorn, drained
50 g/2 oz stuffed green olives, chopped
salt and ground black pepper
15 ml/1 tbsp chopped parsley
milk to glaze

To make the pastry, mix together the flour and salt and rub in the margarine until the mixture resembles fine breadcrumbs. Mix with just enough water to form a firm dough. Cover and chill for at least 30 minutes.

Meanwhile, prepare the filling. Heat the oil in a pan and fry the turkey over moderate heat, turning often, for about 15–20 minutes, until pale golden on all sides. Add the onion and fry for 3 minutes. Leave to cool.

Mix together the soft cheese, sweetcorn and olives, season with salt and pepper and stir in the parsley.

Heat the oven to 200°C/400°F/Gas 6. Grease a baking tray.

Roll out the pastry on a lightly floured surface to make an oblong about 30 by 18 cm/12 by 7 in. Put the cooled turkey along one half of the pastry and cover with the cheese mixture. Moisten the edges of the pastry with water and fold over to enclose the filling completely. Press the edges together to seal and trim to make a neat parcel. Carefully place the pastry, with the seam underneath, on the baking tray and brush with milk. Reroll any trimmings, cut into leaf shapes and arrange in a pattern on the pastry. Brush with milk. Bake for 25–30 minutes, until the pastry is firm.

To serve hot, transfer to a heated serving dish. Or allow to cool slightly, transfer to a wire tray and leave to become cold. Slice thickly.

LAMB AND ARTICHOKES

SERVES 4
Per serving: 310 Cals, 15 g fat, 1 g fibre

550 g/1¼ lb lean lamb
1 large onion, sliced
1 clove garlic, crushed
425 ml/15 fl oz vegetable soup (see page 33)
salt and ground black pepper
400-g/14-oz can artichoke hearts, drained
15 ml/1 tbsp chopped parsley

Heat the oven to 180°C/350°F/Gas 4.

Trim the lamb of any excess fat and cut into 4-cm/1½-in cubes. Fry in a non-stick pan over high heat, stirring, to seal in the juices. Reduce the heat to moderate, add the onion and garlic and stir for 3 minutes. Pour on the soup, season with salt and pepper and bring to the boil.

Transfer to an ovenproof casserole, cover and cook for 1 hour. Add the artichokes and cook for 15 minutes. Stir in the parsley and serve very hot.

Serving suggestion
A mixed green salad, such as lettuce, green pepper and tomato, with an orange dressing; or serve on a bed of long-grain brown rice.

Alternative suggestions
Using home-made vegetable soup as the sauce for a casserole is a good way of adding fibre to a dish, and there's all the difference in the world from using canned soups. Try other soups – carrot, courgette and cauliflower all give good results.

LAMB AND PASTA HOT-POT

SERVES 4
Per serving: 480 Cals, 22 g fat, 2 g fibre

550 g/1¼ lb middle neck of lamb
2 medium-sized onions, sliced
1 clove garlic, crushed
15 ml/1 tbsp 100% wholemeal flour
425 ml/15 fl oz white stock (see page 31)
150 ml/5 fl oz orange juice
salt and ground black pepper
30 ml/2 tbsp chopped mint
100 g/4 oz wholemeal pasta shapes

Heat the oven to 180°C/350°F/Gas 4.

Cut the lamb into cubes and trim off any excess fat. Fry in a non-stick pan over low heat, stirring, until the fat begins to run. Spoon off the excess fat. Slightly increase the heat and cook, turning occasionally until evenly brown. Remove with a draining spoon. Fry the onions in the fat remaining in the pan, stirring to prevent them colouring. Add the garlic and flour, cook for 1 minute, then gradually stir in the stock, then the orange juice. Return the meat to the pan, season with salt and pepper and stir in the mint. Bring to the boil, then transfer to an ovenproof casserole. Cover and cook for 2½ hours.

Meanwhile, cook the pasta in a large pan of boiling, salted water for 12–13 minutes, or according to the directions on the packet, until just tender. Drain thoroughly and stir into the casserole. Cover and return to the oven for 15 minutes.

Serving suggestions
A large bowl of mixed salad – such as shredded hard white cabbage, thinly sliced celery and courgettes and quartered tomatoes – or just a green salad well laced with fresh herbs.

LAMB PILAFF

SERVES 4
Per serving: 410 Cals, 12 g fat, 2 g fibre

425 ml/15 fl oz, plus 30 ml/2 tbsp white stock (see page 31)
225 g/8 oz brown medium-grain rice
salt and ground black pepper
500 g/1 lb lean lamb, trimmed and cut into cubes
1 medium-sized onion, thinly sliced
2 cloves garlic, finely chopped
2 stalks celery, chopped
15 ml/1 tbsp chopped parsley

Garnish:
pinch cayenne pepper

Put 425 ml/15 fl oz stock in a large pan, bring to the boil, add the rice, season with salt and pepper and stir to prevent the rice sticking. Cover and simmer for about 40 minutes, until all the stock has been absorbed and the rice is tender. Remove from the heat.

Meanwhile, fry the lamb in a non-stick pan over low heat until the fat begins to run. Spoon off the excess fat. Increase the heat to moderate, and stir until the meat is sealed on all sides. Stir in the onion, garlic, celery and 30 ml/2 tbsp stock. Cover and simmer very gently, stirring occasionally, for 20 minutes, or until the lamb is tender.

Stir the lamb mixture into the rice, check seasoning and add more if necessary. Stir in the parsley. Transfer to a heated serving dish and sprinkle a little cayenne pepper over to garnish.

STUFFED CABBAGE LEAVES

SERVES 4
Per serving: 240 Cals, 5 g fat, 5 g fibre

8 large cabbage leaves
salt
225 g/8 oz cooked lean lamb, minced
100 g/4 oz cooked brown long-grain rice
45 ml/3 tbsp tomato purée
10 ml/2 tsp German-style mustard
15 ml/1 tbsp chopped mint
ground black pepper
275 ml/½ pint white stock (see page 31)
15 ml/1 tbsp Worcestershire sauce
25 g/1 oz bran
10 ml/2 tsp cornflour

Garnish:
15 ml/1 tbsp chopped parsley

Heat the oven to 180°C/350°F/Gas 4. Grease a shallow ovenproof dish.

Trim the thick stalk ends from the cabbage leaves. Blanch the leaves in boiling, salted water for 2 minutes, drain and pat dry with kitchen paper.

Mix together the lamb, rice, 30 ml/2 tbsp tomato purée, mustard, mint and pepper. Moisten with a very little white stock. Divide between the cabbage leaves and roll up, beginning at the stalk ends and tucking the sides in to make neat parcels. Arrange the rolls in the dish with the 'loose' ends underneath. Pour the stock over, cover and bake for 30 minutes.

Pour off the stock, cover the dish again and keep warm.

Mix together the reserved tomato purée, Worcestershire sauce, bran and cornflour. Gradually stir in a little of the hot stock. Transfer to a small pan, stir in the remaining stock and bring to the boil, stirring. Season well with salt and pepper. Pour a little of the sauce over the cabbage rolls and garnish with the parsley. Serve the rest of the sauce separately.

See photograph on p.105.

GUARD OF HONOUR WITH WALNUT STUFFING

SERVES 4–6

Per serving for 4: 267 Cals,
15 g fat, 5 g fibre

*2 pieces best end of lamb, each
with 6 rib cutlets*

Stuffing:
15 g/½ oz margarine
1 small onion, finely chopped
1 clove garlic, crushed
*100 g/4 oz wholemeal bread-
crumbs*
2 oranges
15 ml/1 tbsp chopped mint
50 g/2 oz walnuts, chopped
salt and ground black pepper
*10 ml/2 tsp 100% wholemeal
flour*
*225 ml/8 fl oz white stock (see
page 31)*
15 ml/1 tbsp chopped parsley

Heat the oven to 180°C/350°F/Gas 4.

Cut away the bony part, or chine, from the meaty end of each joint. Trim the fat from the tips of the bones, leaving 5 cm/2 in bone exposed. Stand the 2 joints upright and facing each other, skin sides outside and bone tips uppermost. Lean the tops of the joints inwards and press them together, so that the bone tips cross. Tie the 2 joints together by weaving string in and out where the bones cross. Cover the bone tips with foil to prevent them from burning.

To make the stuffing, melt the margarine in a small pan and fry the onion and garlic over moderate heat for 3–4 minutes, stirring occasionally, until soft but not brown. Remove from the heat and stir in the breadcrumbs. Grate the rind and squeeze the juice of one orange; divide the other into segments and chop them. Add to the pan with the mint and walnuts and season with salt and pepper. Pack into the V-shaped space between the cutlets. Stand the rack in a roasting tin and roast for 1¾–2 hours, or until the lamb is just cooked, but still slightly pink.

Transfer the meat to a heated serving dish and keep warm. To make the gravy, pour off and reserve the pan juices. Put the roasting pan over moderate heat, sprinkle in the flour and stir with a wooden spoon. Skim off the fat that rises to the top of the pan juices. Pour the remaining juices back into the roasting pan and, still stirring, pour in the stock. Season with salt and pepper and bring to the boil. Serve separately.

Remove the foil from the bone tips and cover them with paper cutlet frills, if you have them. Sprinkle the lamb with the parsley to garnish.

Serving suggestion
Jacket potatoes and a green vegetable such as broccoli or Brussels sprouts topped with 'buttered' crumbs (see page 42).

Alternative suggestions
Other stuffings can be used instead of the walnut stuffing.

SWEET AND SOUR SPAGHETTI

SERVES 6
Per serving: 410 Cals, 9 g fat,
3 g fibre

15 ml/1 tbsp vegetable oil
1 medium-sized onion, sliced
500 g/1 lb pork fillet, thinly
    sliced
30 ml/2 tbsp 100% wholemeal
    flour
30 ml/2 tbsp tomato purée
575 ml/1 pint white stock (see
    page 31)
1 red pepper, trimmed and
    sliced
1 green pepper, trimmed and
    sliced
1 large carrot, cut into match-
    stick strips
100 g/4 oz canned pineapple
    chunks, drained
3 pieces preserved ginger,
    drained and thinly sliced
30 ml/2 tbsp soy sauce
salt and ground black pepper
350 g/12 oz wholemeal
    spaghetti

Heat the oil in a pan and fry the onion over moderate heat for about 3 minutes. Add the pork and cook, stirring frequently for 4–5 minutes, until evenly brown. Stir in the flour, then the tomato purée. Gradually stir in the stock and bring to the boil. Add the peppers and carrot, cover and simmer for 20 minutes, or until the vegetables are just tender. Add the pineapple, ginger and soy sauce, and adjust the seasoning if necessary. Simmer for a further 5 minutes.

Meanwhile, cook the spaghetti in a large pan in plenty of boiling, salted water for 12–13 minutes, or according to the directions on the packet, until just tender. Drain and turn into a greased serving dish. Pour the sauce over and toss, using 2 large forks.

Serving suggestion
Any cool, crisp salad, such as diced cucumber, celery and Chinese leaves.

VEAL BALLS WITH NOODLES

SERVES 4

Per serving: 380 Cals, 5 g fat, 9 g fibre

350 g/12 oz minced stewing veal
1 large onion, finely chopped
1 clove garlic, crushed
100 g/4 oz wholemeal bread-crumbs
5 ml/1 tsp dill seed
15 ml/1 tbsp chopped parsley
salt and ground black pepper
30 ml/2 tbsp 100% wholemeal flour
275 ml/10 fl oz low-fat plain yoghurt
100 g/4 oz mushrooms, sliced
225 g/8 oz wholemeal noodles

Garnish;
15 ml/1 tbsp chopped mint

Fry the veal in a non-stick pan over low heat, stirring, until the fat begins to run. Spoon off the excess fat. Add the onion and garlic and fry over moderate heat, stirring occasionally, for 4–5 minutes, until the onions are transparent. Using a slotted spoon, transfer to a bowl. Stir in the breadcrumbs, dill seed and parsley and season with salt and pepper. Mash well with a fork.

Sprinkle some flour on your hands and shape the mixture into 12 balls. Roll in flour to coat thoroughly. Heat the pan over moderate heat and fry the veal balls in the remaining fat, turning often, until sealed all over. Pour on the yoghurt, cover and simmer for 20 minutes. Season with salt and pepper, add the sliced mushrooms and simmer for 5 minutes.

Meanwhile, cook the noodles in a large pan of boiling, salted water for 12–13 minutes, or according to the directions on the packet, until just tender. Drain thoroughly.

Transfer the veal and sauce to a heated serving dish, arrange the noodles around the outside and sprinkle with the mint.

BEEF AND BEAN POT

SERVES 4

Per serving: 525 Cals, 20 g fat, 19 g fibre

500 g/1 lb stewing beef
40 g/1½ oz 100% wholemeal flour
salt and ground black pepper
2.5 ml/½ tsp mixed dried herbs
15 ml/1 tbsp vegetable oil
1 large onion, sliced
2 cloves garlic, crushed
6 stalks celery, sliced
1 green pepper, trimmed and thinly sliced
225 g/8 oz canned tomatoes
275 ml/½ pint brown stock (see page 32)
15 ml/1 tbsp tomato purée
350 g/12 oz cooked, dried red kidney beans
25 g/1 oz stuffed olives, sliced
25 g/1 oz bran

Heat the oven to 170°C/325°F/Gas 3.

Trim the beef of any excess fat and cut it into 4-cm/1½-in cubes. Toss in the flour seasoned with salt, pepper and the herbs. Heat the oil and fry the beef over moderate heat, a few cubes at a time, until evenly brown. Transfer to an ovenproof casserole.

Fry the onion, garlic, celery and green pepper for 3–4 minutes in the fat remaining in the pan without allowing the vegetables to brown. Stir in the tomatoes, stock and tomato purée and bring to the boil. Pour over the beef and stir well. Cover and cook in the oven for 2 hours. Add the beans, olives and bran and stir well. Cook for a further 45 minutes, or until the beef is tender.

Serving suggestions
Hot, crusty granary rolls and cabbage topped with a few caraway seeds.

Veal balls with noodles (*left*),
Beef and bean pot (*centre*),
Stuffed cabbage leaves (*right*,
see p.101).

BEEF AND RAISIN ROLLS

SERVES 4
Per serving: 425 Cals, 21 g
fat, 9 g fibre

4 thin slices topside of beef
(approx 100 g/4 oz each)
25 g/1 oz margarine
1 small onion, finely chopped
1 clove garlic, crushed
40 g/1½ oz seedless raisins,
chopped
50 g/2 oz wholemeal breadcrumbs
25 g/1 oz bran
15 ml/1 tbsp chopped parsley
2.5 ml/½ tsp mixed spice
salt and ground black pepper
40 g/1½ oz 100% wholemeal
flour

Sauce:
15 ml/1 tbsp vegetable oil
1 medium-sized onion, finely
chopped
1 clove garlic, crushed
25 g/1 oz bran
150 ml/5 fl oz brown stock
(see page 32)
275 ml/½ pint brown ale
40 g/1½ oz raisins

Beat the beef slices between 2 sheets of greaseproof paper until really thin and cut each slice in half. Melt the margarine in a pan and fry the onion and garlic over moderate heat for 3–4 minutes, stirring occasionally, until soft but not coloured. Tip mixture into a bowl and stir in the raisins, breadcrumbs, bran, parsley and spice. Season with salt and pepper and mash with a fork. Spread over the beef slices, pat down firmly and roll up each slice, Swiss-roll fashion. Tie with thin string or twine, or secure with wooden cocktail sticks. Toss in flour to coat thoroughly.

Heat the oven to 170°C/325°F/Gas 3.

To make the sauce, heat the oil in a frying-pan and fry the meat rolls, turning occasionally, until evenly brown. Transfer to an ovenproof casserole. Fry the onion and garlic in the fat remaining in the pan for 3–4 minutes, stirring occasionally. Add any remaining flour and the bran and stir well. Gradually stir in the stock and ale, add the raisins, season with salt and pepper and bring to the boil, stirring. Pour over the meat rolls, cover and bake for 2 hours. Remove the string or cocktail sticks. Sprinkle with parsley and serve hot.

Garnish:
15 ml/1 tbsp chopped parsley

BEEF COBBLER

SERVES 4
Per serving: 425 Cals, 22 g
fat, 7 g fibre

500 g/1 lb minced beef
1 large onion, chopped
30 ml/2 tbsp 100% wholemeal
flour
400 g/14 oz canned tomatoes
15 ml/1 tbsp tomato purée
100 g/4 oz button mushrooms
5 ml/1 tsp mixed dried herbs
salt and ground black pepper

Topping:
4 slices wholemeal bread
spread with margarine

Heat the oven to 200°C/400°F/Gas 6.

Put the minced beef into a non-stick frying-pan and stir over low heat until the fat begins to run. Spoon off the excess fat. Raise the heat to moderate and fry, stirring frequently, to brown the meat evenly. Remove the meat with a slotted spoon and set aside.

Fry the onion in the fat remaining in the pan for 3–4 minutes. Return the meat to the pan, add the flour and stir for 1 minute. Add the tomatoes, tomato purée, mushrooms, dried herbs and bring to the boil. Season with salt and pepper, and simmer for 10 minutes. Transfer to an ovenproof dish.

Cut the bread into triangles and arrange 'buttered' side up, on the meat. Bake for 15–20 minutes until the topping is golden and crisp.

RABBIT STEW WITH HERB DUMPLINGS

SERVES 4

Per serving: 520 Cals, 22 g fat, 7 g fibre

15 g/½ oz margarine
1 large onion, sliced
4 stalks celery, sliced
1 kg/2¼ lb rabbit pieces
25 g/1 oz 100% wholemeal flour
salt and ground black pepper
225 g/8 oz carrots, sliced
225 g/8 oz very small potatoes, scrubbed
275 ml/½ pint dry cider
275 ml/½ pint white stock (see page 31)
15 ml/1 tbsp whole-grain mustard
100 g/4 oz mushrooms, sliced

Dumplings:
100 g/4 oz 100% wholemeal flour
10 ml/2 tsp baking powder
2.5 ml/½ tsp salt
50 g/2 oz margarine
5 ml/1 tsp mixed dried herbs
approx 60 ml/4 tbsp milk

Heat the margarine in a large pan and fry the onion over moderate heat for about 3 minutes without browning. Add the celery and fry for 2 minutes. Toss the rabbit in flour seasoned with salt and pepper and add to the pan. Fry for 5 minutes, turning frequently so that the meat browns evenly. Add the carrots, cider, stock and mustard and bring to the boil. Taste and season with salt and pepper if necessary. Cover and simmer gently for 1½ hours.

Meanwhile make the dumplings. Mix together the flour, baking powder and salt and rub in the margarine until the mixture resembles fine breadcrumbs. Add the herbs and just enough milk to make a soft dough. Roll the dough between your hands to shape into 8 balls. Add to the pan with the mushrooms and potatoes. Cover again and simmer for 15–20 minutes, until the dumplings are light and risen.

Serving suggestion

Root vegetables are the traditional accompaniment to a poacher's stew of this kind – parsnips, turnips, swedes, carrots, either served separately or mixed. If serving a medley of vegetables, make them more interesting by preparing them in different shapes – sliced, diced, short, stubby matchsticks, and so on. Garnish with chopped mint.

6 BAKING

Home cooks unused to baking with wholemeal flour will find that it produces some exciting differences:

Wholemeal flour has its own 'nutty' taste, and therefore adds extra flavour to your baking.

Breads, cakes, biscuits and scones do not rise so much, so will have a closer, slightly heavier texture.

Pastries will also be slightly heavier. Throughout the book there is a selection of pastry recipes – get used to using them with all your favourite fillings.

Choosing wholemeal flour, which contains the whole of the *cleaned* wheatgrain – including the bran and the wheat germ, or embryo – adds to the intake of dietary fibre, iron and the B group vitamins.

Flours are referred to by their extraction rate. Wholemeal (or wholewheat) flour is termed 100%, signifying that nothing has been taken away. It can be coarse, medium or fine, according to the grinding process, and 100% self-raising flour has baking powder added.

Flours with some of the outer husk, the bran, removed – and therefore giving lighter results – are described by the percentage remaining – 81%, 85%, and so on.

To make your own 'extraction rate' flour, use a large metal sieve to remove the bran, which can then be used in other ways.

To convert either commercial or home-made 81% extraction rate flour to self-raising flour, add 25 g/1 oz baking powder to each 450 g/1 lb.

White flours usually contain only 70–72% of the cleaned wheat grain, and therefore much less fibre.

Avoid flours which are simply called 'brown' or 'wheatmeal', for example, as the terms are meaningless and too vague to be informative.

You will find that baking with wholemeal flour produces bread, cakes and biscuits that are more filling and therefore more satisfying – in other words, you actually eat less.

If it seems unrealistic to cut out sugar entirely in your baking, try to cut it down to the minimum. Choose the plainer breads, cakes and biscuits for everyday meals and serve the sweeter recipes only in a selection for special occasions. One slice of gingerbread once in a while never hurt anybody!

BASIC WHOLEMEAL BREAD

MAKES 4 × 450-g/1-lb LOAVES
Per 50-g/2-oz slice: 130 Cals,
1 g fat, 4 g fibre

This is a basic recipe for
wholemeal bread. The
amounts of sugar, fat and
salt can be varied according
to individual taste, and the
amount of water that the
flour will take up will vary
according to the particular
flour you are using.

*850 ml/1½ pints water at
    43°C/110°F (see method)
25 g/1 oz sugar
25 g/1 oz dried yeast
25 g/1 oz margarine
15 ml/1 tbsp salt
1.4 kg/3 lb 100% wholemeal
    flour*

To obtain the correct temperature of water, mix together one-third boiling water with two-thirds cold water from the tap.

Measure 100 ml/3½ fl oz of boiling water and 175 ml/6 fl oz cold water (one-third of the total quantity required) into a bowl. Dissolve half the sugar in the water, add the yeast and whisk with a fork. Leave to stand in a warm place for 10–15 minutes, until it becomes frothy.

Meanwhile, in a large warmed bowl, rub the fat into the salt, flour and remaining sugar. Make a well in the centre.

When the yeast is frothy, mix 200 ml/7 fl oz boiling water and 375 ml/13 fl oz cold water (the remaining water). Pour into the flour with the yeast liquid. Mix thoroughly until the dough is smooth and leaves the sides of the bowl clean.

Turn the dough on to a lightly floured surface and knead for 10 minutes. To do this, fold the dough towards you, then push down and away with the palm of the hand.

Wrap loosely in greased polythene and leave it in a warm place to rise until doubled in size. The time will depend on the temperature of the kitchen. In a warm place it could be as little as 30 minutes; at average room temperature, 1–2 hours; and in the refrigerator – when the dough is made the day before baking – 12–24 hours.

To make 4 loaves, grease 4 × 450-g/1-lb loaf tins and put in a warm place. Alternatively, you can shape the bread and bake on baking trays (see page 114).

Set the oven at the highest temperature so that it has reached its maximum heat when the bread is ready.

When the dough has doubled in size, turn on to the lightly floured working surface and knead gently for 3–4 minutes. Divide into 4 pieces. Flatten each into an oblong the same width as the tin. Fold in 3, smooth the top, tuck in the ends, and place in the tin. Cover the tin and leave in a warm place to rise again, for about 30 minutes, or until the dough has risen 1.5 cm/½ in above the top of the tins. If the dough springs back when pressed with a lightly floured finger, it is ready to bake.

The loaves can be glazed or decorated before baking to give them a variety of finishes (see page 112).

Turn down the oven to 230°C/450°F/Gas 9 and bake for 30–40 minutes, or until the loaves shrink slightly from the sides of the tins. If they brown too quickly, reduce the heat to 220°C/425°F/Gas 7 after 20 minutes. When the loaves are cooked, they should sound hollow when tapped underneath with the knuckles. Turn out and leave on a wire rack to cool.

To use fresh yeast
Use 50 g/2 oz fresh yeast for the given quantity of flour.
    Mix together the flour and salt and rub in the fat. Stir in the sugar. Cream the yeast in a little water and set aside in a warm place for a few minutes until it froths. Add the yeast mixture and the remaining water to the flour mixture all at once. Mix quickly until the dough leaves the sides of the bowl. Then continue as described.

To make bread more quickly
Single rising   The dough can be shaped after the first kneading and left to rise, just once. This gives a loaf with a coarser texture.

Ascorbic acid (Vitamin C)   If this is included in the recipe, not only is a single rising sufficient, but the dough rises quickly and has a light texture.

1 × 50-mg tablet ascorbic acid (Vitamin C)
15 ml/1 tbsp sugar
25 g/1 oz dried yeast
850 ml/1½ pints warm water
1.4 kg/3 lb 100% wholemeal flour
25 g/1 oz margarine
15 ml/1 tbsp salt

Crush the ascorbic acid tablet in a small bowl. Add 5 ml/1 tsp sugar and all the yeast. Measure one-third of the required quantity of warm water, pour into the bowl and whisk with a fork. Leave in a warm place for 10–15 minutes, until it becomes frothy.
    Grease 4 × 450-g/1-lb loaf tins, or 2 baking trays, according to the type of loaves you wish to make.
    Reserve a cupful of flour and tip the rest into a large bowl. Rub in the margarine. Stir in the remaining sugar and the salt and pour on the yeast liquid and the remaining water. Mix thoroughly until the dough is smooth enough to leave the sides of the bowl. Sprinkle some flour from the cup on to a working surface and rub some on to your hands. Turn out the dough and knead for about 10 minutes, using some flour from the

cup if it becomes too sticky, until the dough is smooth and elastic.

Shape the dough as required (see page 114). Cover the tins or baking trays and leave in a warm place for about 30 minutes to rise, until doubled in size.

Meanwhile, turn the oven to its highest setting.

When the dough has risen, reduce the temperature to 230°C/450°F/Gas 8 and bake for 30–35 minutes. If the bread browns too quickly, lower the heat after 20 minutes to 220°C/425°F/Gas 7. Test the bread by tapping the underside with your knuckles. It should sound hollow.

Bran-plus bread
For an extra high-fibre bread, stir 40 g/1½ oz bran into each 450 g/1 lb 100% wholemeal flour before rubbing in the margarine.

Glazes
With these you can vary the crust on your loaves.

Soft crust Dust the loaf with flour before baking. Wrap the baked loaf in a cloth while cooling.

Crisp crust Brush the risen dough lightly with water, or salt and water.

Shiny crust Brush the risen dough lightly with milk or, not quite so shiny, a mixture of milk and water.

Golden brown crust Brush the risen dough with 1 egg, or egg yolk, beaten with a little milk, or with melted margarine.

Toppings
Wholemeal or rye flour, sifted or not, bran, Bran Flakes, crushed wheat flakes, cracked (or kibbled) wheat, fine or medium oatmeal, oat flakes, rolled oats, poppy seeds, or other spice seeds – fennel, aniseed, caraway, cumin, sesame, dill or coriander – can all be sprinkled on to loaves to add interest and variety. Seeds will stay in place better if the dough is first brushed with a glaze.

Cottage loaf (*left,* **see p.114**),
Dinner twists (*centre,* **see p.114**),
Flowerpot loaf (*top right,* **see p.114**), **Plaited loaf** (*bottom right,* **see p.114**).

Shapes

Cottage loaf Divide the dough in half and then each half into 2 pieces, one twice the size of the other. Shape each piece into a round. Press one small piece on top of a large one. Press a floured finger or the handle of a wooden spoon through the centre, from the top, to join the 2 sections. Repeat with the remaining dough.

Plaited loaf Divide the dough in half. Divide one half into 3 pieces and shape each into a roll about 30 cm/12 long. Press the 3 pieces together at one end and place on a greased baking tray. Place a rolling pin or other heavy weight over the joined ends to keep the dough steady. Plait the 3 pieces loosely together to allow for the dough to rise. (Remember – right over left and under, left over right and under.) Taper the ends slightly and press them firmly together. Repeat with the remaining dough.

Bloomer Divide the dough into 3 and shape each piece into a thick roll about 15 cm/6 in long. Place on a greased baking tray, cut 3 diagonal slashes in each with a knife, cover and leave to rise as usual.

Coburg Divide the dough into 4 and shape each piece into a round – or 'cob' – shape. Cut a deep cross through the centre. Repeat with the other 3 pieces. Place on a baking tray, cover and leave to rise as usual.

Flowerpot loaf Bread can actually be baked in new, or scrupulously clean earthenware flowerpots. First grease them well and bake them unfilled, at 200°C/400°F/Gas 6 for 30 minutes. Repeat once more and the pots are ready for bread. (If this initial preparation is omitted, the bread will stick.)

To use the flowerpots for baking, grease well and then treat just as any other tin or ovenproof dish. Stand the pots upright in

the oven for baking.

Similarly shaped loaves, narrow at the base, can be made by baking the dough in ovenproof bowls.

Round rolls Cut the dough into small pieces, slightly larger than a golf ball. Roll each into a ball with the palm of the hand, pressing down and then easing up as the dough forms a smooth ball. Arrange well apart on baking trays, cover and leave to rise as usual.

Bake the rolls at 230°C/450°F/Gas 8 for 15–20 minutes until well risen and hollow-sounding.

Crown loaf Shape 10 round rolls. Grease a 25-cm/10-in cake tin and arrange 7 rolls round the outside and 3 in the centre. Cover with greased polythene and leave to rise as usual. Brush with a milk glaze and scatter with poppy seeds.

Alternatively, arrange 6 round rolls in 2 rows in a 450-g/1-lb loaf tin.

Dinner twists Divide the dough into small pieces about 40 g/1½ oz each and shape into a 20-cm/8-in sausage, about 2.5 cm/1 in in diameter.

Either twist into a letter 'S' shape; or twist into a horseshoe shape and fold the ends into the sides; or tie a loose knot in the centre of each strip; or roll a strip round into a wheel. Place well apart on a greased baking tray. Cover and leave to rise as usual. Bake as for round rolls.

Freezing bread
Bread freezes perfectly, so if you have a freezer it makes sense to make a large batch on the 'some for now, some for later' principle.

Unrisen dough After the first kneading, cut the dough into suitable quantities – 450 g/1 lb dough for a small loaf. Place in a large, greased polythene bag, expel the air and seal, leaving space for the dough to rise a little before it freezes. It can be frozen for up to 8 weeks.

To use, loosen the bag and leave the dough to thaw and rise at room temperature. Knead and shape as required.

Risen dough Prepare to the second kneading stage. Divide into loaf-sized portions, shape as you wish, and wrap individually in lightly greased polythene. Tie firmly, label and freeze. Can be frozen for 2–3 weeks. To use, transfer the frozen dough to a greased baking tray, cover and leave to thaw and rise at room temperature.

Baked bread Allow to cool completely, then wrap tightly in polythene. Most types of bread can be stored for about 4–6 months, but loaves and rolls with very crisp crusts – French loaves, for example – shed the crust after only 2–3 days.

One way to be sure of a fresh slice of bread for breakfast every day: slice a loaf, pack it, still in its loaf shape, in polythene, fast-freeze and take out just as many slices as you need. The bread thaws very quickly at room temperature, or can be toasted without thawing.

Fresh yeast Can be frozen in handy amounts, e.g. 25 g/1 oz yeast. If grated while frozen, it can be used straight from the freezer or it can be thawed for 30 minutes at room temperature. As yeast loses some of its power during freezing allow 50% more than is normally used. It can be frozen for up to 6 months.

WHOLEMEAL PLAIT

MAKES 1 × 900-g/2-lb LOAF
Per loaf: 2,345 Cals, 43 g fat, 76 g fibre

5 ml/1 tsp sugar
425 ml/15 fl oz warm water (see page 110)
15 ml/1 tbsp dried yeast
550 g/1 lb 4 oz 100% wholemeal flour
5 ml/1 tsp salt
45 ml/3 tbsp bran
25 g/1 oz margarine
milk to glaze
15 ml/1 tbsp poppy seeds or sesame seeds (optional)

Dissolve the sugar in 150 ml/5 fl oz of the warm water. Sprinkle on the yeast, stir well and leave in a warm place for 10–15 minutes to become frothy.

Mix together the flour and salt, stir in the bran and rub in the margarine. Make a well in the centre and pour in the yeast liquid and remaining warm water. Mix to a firm dough that leaves the sides of the bowl clean.

Turn on to a lightly floured surface and knead for about 10 minutes, until smooth and elastic. Cover loosely with greased polythene and leave in a warm place until doubled in size. Turn out and knead lightly for 3–4 minutes.

Heat the oven to 220°C/425°F/Gas 7. Grease and warm a baking tray.

Divide into 3 and shape into a plait (see page 114). Brush with milk and sprinkle with poppy or sesame seeds if used. Place on the baking tray.

Bake for 25 minutes, then reduce the heat to 190°C/375°F/Gas 5 and continue baking for a further 15–20 minutes, or until the loaf sounds hollow when tapped underneath with the knuckles.

RYE RING LOAF

MAKES 1 × 800-g/1¾-lb LOAF
Per loaf: 2,426 Cals, 61 g fat,
67 g fibre

50 g/2 oz margarine
250 ml/9 fl oz warm water
(see page 110)
25 g/1 oz fresh yeast
300 g/11 oz 100% wholemeal
flour
300 g/11 oz rye flour
10 ml/2 tsp salt
5 ml/1 tsp ground coriander
30 ml/2 tbsp chopped fresh
herbs (such as marjoram,
parsley, thyme)
15 ml/1 tbsp poppy seeds

Gently heat the margarine and water until the margarine has melted. Put the yeast into a small bowl and cream it with a little of the warm liquid. Set aside in a warm place for 15 minutes, until bubbly.

Mix together the flours, salt, coriander and herbs. Make a well in the centre and pour on the yeast liquid and remaining warm liquid. Mix to a firm dough.

Turn out on to a lightly floured surface and knead for about 10 minutes, until smooth. Wrap loosely in greased polythene and leave in a warm place to double in size.

Grease and warm a baking tray.

Knead the dough lightly and shape into a long sausage. Wrap round to form a ring and pinch the 2 ends to make a neat join. Place on baking tray, cover loosely with greased polythene and leave in a warm place for about 30 minutes.

Heat the oven to 220°C/425°F/Gas 7.

Scatter poppy seeds over the ring and make a few slits in the top all around. Bake for 30–35 minutes until firm and well risen.

RYE BAPS

MAKES 4 LARGE BAPS
Per bap: 660 Cals, 7 g fat, 21 g fibre

375 ml/13 fl oz warm milk
and water, mixed (see page
110)
5 ml/1 tsp sugar
15 g/½ oz dried yeast
375 g/13 oz rye flour
375 g/13 oz 100% wholemeal
flour
5 ml/1 tsp salt

Pour half of the warm milk and water into a small bowl, stir in the sugar to dissolve, then sprinkle on the yeast. Set aside in a warm place for 10–15 minutes until frothy.

Mix together the flours and salt and make a well in the centre. Pour in the yeast liquid and the remaining milk mixture, and stir to form a dough. Turn on to a lightly floured surface and knead for about 10 minutes, until smooth. Wrap loosely in greased polythene and leave in a warm place to double in size.

Grease and warm a baking tray.

Lightly knead the dough for 3–4 minutes and divide into 4 pieces. Roll out each piece on a lightly floured board and place on the baking tray. Loosely cover with greased polythene and leave in a warm place for 30 minutes.

Heat the oven to 230°C/450°F/Gas 8.

Lightly sprinkle the tops with rye flour. Bake for 15–20 minutes, until crisp. (They do not rise very much.)

Rye baps (*above and left*), **Rye ring loaf** (*right*).

KIBBLED WHEAT LOAF

MAKES 1 × 700-g/1½-lb LOAF
Per loaf: 1,629 Cals, 25 g fat,
43 g fibre

5 ml/1 tsp sugar
275 ml/½ pint warm water
  (see page 110)
15 g/½ oz dried yeast
350 g/12 oz 100% wholemeal
  flour
100 g/4 oz cracked wheat
5 ml/1 tsp salt
15 g/½ oz margarine
milk and water to glaze

Decoration:
extra cracked wheat

Dissolve the sugar in half the water and sprinkle on the yeast. Leave in a warm place for 10–15 minutes, until frothy.

Mix together the flour, wheat and salt and rub in the margarine. Make a well in the centre and pour on the yeast liquid and remaining warm water. Mix to a firm dough that leaves the sides of the bowl clean. Turn on to a lightly floured surface and knead for 10 minutes, until smooth.

Wrap loosely in greased polythene and leave in a warm place until doubled in size.

Heat the oven to 230°C/450°F/Gas 8. Grease and warm a baking tray.

Knead the dough for 3–4 minutes and shape into a large round. Place on the warmed baking tray, cover loosely with greased polythene and leave in a warm place until doubled in size.

Score the top into 8 wedges. Brush with milk and water and sprinkle with cracked wheat. Bake for 35–40 minutes, or until the loaf sounds hollow when tapped underneath.

OAT PLAIT

MAKES 1 × 1.1-kg/2½-lb LOAF
Per loaf: 1,755 Cals, 32 g fat,
41 g fibre

5 ml/1 tsp sugar
150 ml/5 fl oz warm water
  (see page 110)
10 ml/2 tsp dried yeast
275 g/10 oz 100% wholemeal
  flour
175 g/6 oz rolled oats
10 ml/2 tsp salt
5 ml/1 tsp vegetable oil
approx 150 ml/5 fl oz warm
  milk
milk to glaze

Decoration:
rolled oats

Dissolve the sugar in the water then sprinkle on the yeast. Leave in a warm place for 10–15 minutes until frothy. Mix together the flour, oats and salt, make a well in the centre and pour in the yeast liquid and the oil. Stir well, then gradually pour in the milk, using just enough to give a soft but not sticky dough.

Turn the dough on to a lightly floured surface and knead for about 10 minutes, until smooth and elastic. Wrap loosely in greased polythene and leave in a warm place until doubled in size.

Heat the oven to 200°C/400°F/Gas 6. Grease and warm a baking tray.

Turn the dough on to a lightly floured surface and knead it for about 5 minutes.

Divide the dough into 3 and shape into a plait (see page 114). Place on the baking tray, cover loosely with greased polythene and leave in a warm place until doubled in size. Brush with milk and sprinkle with a few oats. Bake for about 30 minutes, or until the loaf sounds hollow when tapped underneath.

SOURDOUGH ROLLS

MAKES 18 ROLLS
Per roll: 100 Cals, 1 g fat, 6 g fibre

Start the day ahead of baking.

1 recipe sourdough 'starter' (see below)
450 g/1 lb rye flour
15 g/½ oz fresh yeast
450 ml/16 fl oz warm water (see page 110)
5 ml/1 tsp salt
milk to glaze
15 ml/1 tbsp poppy seeds

Place half the flour in a bowl. Cream the yeast with 30 ml/2 tbsp of the warm water. Pour on the remaining water and mix well. Pour the yeast liquid and the 'starter' into the flour and knead until smooth. Cover the bowl and leave in a warm place overnight.

Mix together the remaining flour and the salt and sprinkle on to the dough. Knead until all the flour is taken up and the dough is smooth.

Heat the oven to 230°C/450°F/Gas 8. Grease and warm a baking tray.

Divide the dough into 18 pieces and shape into rolls. Place on the baking tray, brush with milk and cut a cross shape in the top of each. Sprinkle with poppy seeds. Leave in a warm place until doubled in size.

Bake for 20 minutes, or until well risen and crispy.

SOURDOUGH 'STARTER'

Takes 2 days to work

15 ml/1 tbsp milk
30 ml/2 tbsp water
15 ml/1 tbsp warm water (see page 110)
5 ml/1 tsp sugar
2.5 ml/½ tsp dried yeast
5 ml/1 tsp salt
50 g/2 oz 100% wholemeal flour

Put the milk and 30 ml/2 tbsp water into a small pan. Bring to the boil, then remove from the heat. Put the 15 ml/1 tbsp warm water into a small bowl, stir in the sugar to dissolve, then sprinkle on the yeast. Leave in a warm place for 10 minutes until frothy. Mix with the milk and water and stir in the salt. Put the flour into a bowl, pour on the liquid all at once and stir well. Cover and leave in a warm place for 1 day.

If you make twice the quantity, it will stay 'alive' for future use if the bowl is covered and kept at room temperature. Do not chill.

WHOLEMEAL SODA BREAD

MAKES 2 × 300-g/11-oz LOAVES
Per loaf: 885 Cals, 10 g fat, 24 g fibre

500 g/1 lb 2 oz 100% wholemeal flour
10 ml/2 tsp salt
5 ml/1 tsp bicarbonate of soda
275 ml/½ pint milk
5 ml/1 tsp lemon juice
approx 30 ml/2 tbsp warm water

Heat the oven to 220°C/425°F/Gas 7. Flour a baking tray.

Sift together the flour, salt and soda and add the bran remaining in the sieve. Mix together the milk and lemon juice, stir into the flour and mix to a firm dough, adding a little warm water if necessary. Divide in 2, shape each into a round and place on the baking tray. Cover each with a deep inverted cake tin and bake near the top of the oven for 30 minutes. Remove the covering tins and bake for about 15 minutes, or until firm.

Serve warm and preferably on the day of baking.

SPICED PUMPKIN BREAD

MAKES 1 × 450-g/1-lb LOAF
Per loaf: 1,145 Cals, 38 g fat,
27 g fibre

225-g/8-oz pumpkin, peeled
and diced (or 175 ml/6 fl oz
canned pumpkin)
25 g/1 oz margarine
2.5 ml/½ tsp ground cinnamon
2.5 ml/½ tsp ground ginger
pinch grated nutmeg
5 ml/1 tsp sugar
15 ml/1 tbsp warm water (see
page 110)
1 egg, beaten
15 g/½ oz dried yeast
225 g/8 oz 100% wholemeal
flour
10 ml/2 tsp salt
milk to glaze
15 ml/1 tbsp sesame seeds

Steam the pumpkin for 20–25 minutes, or until tender. Mash thoroughly and, while still hot, beat in the margarine and spices. Leave to cool.

In a small bowl, beat together the sugar, water and egg, sprinkle on the yeast and leave in a warm place for 10–15 minutes, until frothy.

In a large bowl, mix together the flour and salt, make a well in the centre and pour in the yeast liquid and pumpkin purée (and margarine and spices if using canned pumpkin). Stir well and knead for 5 minutes, until the dough is smooth and leaves the sides of the bowl. Wrap loosely in greased polythene and leave in a warm place until doubled in size.

Heat the oven to 200°C/400°F/Gas 6. Grease and warm a baking tray.

Turn out the dough and knead lightly for 3–4 minutes. Shape into a round and place on the prepared baking tray. Cover loosely with greased polythene and leave in a warm place to double in size.

Bake for 30 minutes. Remove from the oven, brush with milk and sprinkle with the sesame seeds. Return to the oven for 10 minutes, or until the loaf is firm and the top crusty.

Serving suggestions
Serve sliced and spread with low-fat soft cheese, or slightly warm to accompany a dessert of fresh fruit salad.

DAIRY BREAD

MAKES 1 × 900-g/2-lb LOAF
Per loaf: 2,700 Cals, 114 g fat,
25 g fibre

350 g/12 oz 81% wheatmeal
self-raising flour (see page
108)
5 ml/1 tsp salt
10 ml/2 tsp mustard powder
pinch cayenne pepper
100 g/4 oz soft margarine
75 g/3 oz Edam cheese, grated
275 ml/½ pint buttermilk
1 egg
5 ml/1 tsp lightly crushed
fennel seeds (optional)

Heat the oven to 190°C/375°F/Gas 5. Line a 900-g/2-lb loaf tin with greased foil.

Sift together the flour, salt, mustard and cayenne pepper and add any bran remaining in the sieve. Beat in the margarine, cheese, buttermilk and egg and beat for 1–2 minutes, until smooth. Turn into the loaf tin, smooth the top and sprinkle with the seeds. Bake for 45 minutes, or until springy.

Serving suggestions
Serve warm with soup, or cheese and celery sticks.

POTATO WHOLEMEAL BREAD

MAKES 2 × 450-g/1-lb LOAVES
Per loaf: 1,300 Cals, 18 g fat,
35 g fibre

225 g/8 oz potatoes
2.5 ml/½ tsp sugar
25 g/1 oz margarine
15 g/½ oz fresh yeast
700 g/1½ lb 100% wholemeal
  flour
10 ml/2 tsp salt

Boil the potatoes, then drain and reserve the water. Mash or sieve until completely smooth, then stir in the sugar and margarine and 275 ml/½ pint of the reserved hot cooking water. When well blended, leave to cool. Crumble in the yeast, stir well and leave in a warm place for 10 minutes, until bubbly. Gradually stir in the flour and salt to make a soft dough and mix until it is smooth enough to leave the sides of the bowl. Knead for about 10 minutes until smooth and elastic. Wrap loosely in greased polythene and leave in a warm place until doubled in size.

Heat the oven to 230°C/450°F/Gas 8. Grease and warm 2 × 450-g/1-lb loaf tins.

Turn out the dough and knead again until it is smooth. Shape the dough into the loaf tins (see page 110), cover loosely with greased polythene and leave in a warm place until doubled in size.

Bake for 15 minutes, reduce the heat to 190°C/375°F/Gas 5 and continue baking for 45 minutes, or until the loaves sound hollow when tapped.

Serving suggestions
This bread is very good with cheese and crisp pickled vegetables or with cold meat and chutney.

WHEAT GERM BREAD

MAKES 1 × 900-g/2-lb LOAF
Per loaf: 3,360 Cals, 53 g fat,
51 g fibre

25 g/1 oz margarine
275 ml/½ pint milk (or milk
  and water)
1 egg
50 g/2 oz wheat germ
30 ml/2 tbsp cracked wheat
40 g/1½ oz brown sugar
50 g/2 oz 81% wheatmeal
  self-raising flour (see page
  108)
175 g/6 oz 100% wholemeal
  flour
15 ml/1 tbsp baking powder
2.5 ml/½ tsp bicarbonate of
  soda
15 ml/1 tsp salt

Heat the oven to 180°C/350°F/Gas 4.

Line a 900-g/2-lb loaf tin with greased foil.

Gently melt the margarine in the milk. Remove from the heat and beat in the egg, wheat germ, cracked wheat and sugar. Leave to cool.

Sift together the flours, baking powder, soda and salt and add any bran remaining in the sieve. Make a well in the centre and stir in the milk mixture. Turn into the tin and level the top, sprinkle with a little wholemeal flour and bake for 45–50 minutes.

Serving suggestion
This is delicious served warm with cheese, celery and radishes and other crunchy salad vegetables.

ONION AND TOMATO TEABREAD

MAKES 2 × 450-g/1-lb LOAVES
Per loaf: 560 Cals, 18 g fat,
10 g fibre

225 g/8 oz 81% wheatmeal
self-raising flour (see page
108)
2.5 ml/½ tsp salt
ground black pepper
2.5 ml/½ tsp mustard powder
25 g/1 oz margarine
15 ml/1 tbsp grated onion
2 medium-sized tomatoes,
skinned, seeded and chopped
15 ml/1 tbsp chopped parsley
1 egg
150 ml/5 fl oz milk

Heat the oven to 190°C/375°F/Gas 5. Grease 2 × 450-g/1-lb loaf tins.

Sift together the flour, salt, pepper and mustard powder and add any bran remaining in the sieve. Rub in the margarine until the mixture resembles fine breadcrumbs. Stir in the onion, chopped tomato and parsley. Beat together the egg and milk and pour on to the dry ingredients. Mix to a stiff batter and spoon into the tins. Bake for 30–40 minutes, until well risen and golden brown. Transfer to a wire rack to cool.

Serving suggestions
Serve with soup, salad, or cheese.

HONEY FRUIT LOAF

MAKES 1 × 450-g/1-lb LOAF
Per loaf: 1,470 Cals, 18 g fat,
55 g fibre

175 g/6 oz 100% wholemeal
flour
2.5 ml/½ tsp salt
15 ml/1 tbsp honey
15 ml/1 tbsp black treacle
150 ml/5 fl oz milk
2.5 ml/½ tsp bicarbonate of
soda
50 g/2 oz sultanas
50 g/2 oz seedless raisins

Heat the oven to 170°C/325°F/Gas 3. Grease a 450-g/1-lb loaf tin.

Mix together the flour and salt and make a well in the centre.

Gently melt the honey, treacle and half the milk. Dissolve the soda in the remaining milk and mix with the other milk mixture. Pour into the flour and stir in the fruit. Turn into the tin. Bake for 1½–1¾ hours, until a skewer pierced through the centre of the loaf comes out clean.

SPICED TREACLE LOAF

MAKES 1 × 450-g/1-lb LOAF
Per loaf: 1,230 Cals, 37 g fat,
24 g fibre

5 ml/1 tsp sugar
150 ml/5 fl oz warm water
  (see page 110)
10 ml/2 tsp dried yeast
225 g/8 oz 100% wholemeal
  flour
pinch salt
15 g/½ oz margarine
45 ml/3 tbsp black treacle
25 g/1 oz margarine, melted
10 ml/2 tsp ground ginger
15 ml/1 tbsp melted honey to
  glaze

Dissolve the sugar in the water, then sprinkle on the yeast. Leave in a warm place for 10–15 minutes, or until frothy.

Mix together the flour and salt and rub in the margarine. Make a well in the centre and pour in the yeast liquid. Mix until the dough is pliable and leaves the sides of the bowl clean.

Turn on to a lightly floured surface and knead for 10 minutes. Wrap loosely in greased polythene and leave in a warm place until doubled in size.

Heat the oven to 200°C/400°F/Gas 6. Grease and warm a 450-g/1-lb loaf tin.

Turn the dough into a large bowl, add the treacle, margarine and ginger and mix until the mixture is smooth and no longer sticky.

Turn into the loaf tin and smooth the top. Cover loosely with greased polythene and leave in a warm place until the dough reaches the top of the tin.

Bake for 30–35 minutes. Remove from the oven, stand on a wire rack and brush the top with the melted honey.

FIG LOAF

MAKES 1 × 900-g/2-lb LOAF
Per loaf: 1,470 Cals, 18 g fat,
55 g fibre

100 g/4 oz All-Bran
100 g/4 oz brown sugar
30 ml/2 tbsp black treacle
100 g/4 oz dried figs, chopped
275 ml/½ pint milk
100 g/4 oz 81% wheatmeal
  self-raising flour (see page
  108)
2.5 ml/½ tsp ground ginger

Heat the oven to 180°C/350°F/Gas 4. Grease a 900-g/2-lb loaf tin.

Soak the All-Bran, sugar, treacle and figs in the milk for 30 minutes, until the milk has been absorbed. Mix together the flour and ginger and stir into the fruit mixture. Turn into the tin.

Bake for 45–55 minutes, until a skewer pierced through the centre comes out clean.

Alternative suggestion
Replace the figs with 100 g/4 oz chopped dried apricots, and the ground ginger with mixed spice.

See photograph on p.124.

123

HERB BREAD

MAKES 8 SLICES
Per slice: 230 Cals, 6 g fat, 6 g fibre

450 g/1 lb 100% wholemeal
flour
5 ml/1 tsp salt
ground black pepper
7.5 ml/1½ tsp bicarbonate of
soda
25 g/1 oz margarine
2 medium-sized onions, grated
1 clove garlic, crushed
5 ml/1 tsp mixed dried herbs
5 ml/1 tsp chopped parsley
200 ml/7 fl oz milk
10 ml/2 tsp lemon juice
25 g/1 oz Cheddar cheese,
grated

Heat the oven to 200°C/400°F/Gas 6. Flour a baking tray.

Sift together the flour, salt, pepper and soda and add any bran remaining in the sieve. Rub in the margarine until the mixture resembles fine breadcrumbs. Stir in the onion, garlic and herbs. Mix together the milk and lemon juice, stir into the dry ingredients and mix to a soft dough. Turn on to a lightly floured surface and knead lightly until smooth. Shape into a 23-cm/9-in round and place on the baking tray. Score the top into 8 segments, brush with milk and sprinkle with cheese. Bake for 30–35 minutes, until well risen and golden brown.

Serving suggestions
Serve warm with soup and salad for an informal lunch, or with cheese and a tomato salad for a light supper. It is best eaten on the day it is made.

BRAN FRUIT LOAF

MAKES 1 × 900-g/2-lb LOAF
Per loaf: 1,819 Cals, 18 g fat, 53 g fibre

100 g/4 oz All-Bran
110 g/4 oz brown sugar
100 g/4 oz saltanas
100 g/4 oz currants
50 g/2 oz seedless raisins
275 ml/½ pint milk
100 g/4 oz 81% wheatmeal
self-raising flour (see
page 108)

Heat the oven to 180°C/350°F/Gas 4. Grease a 900-g/2-lb loaf tin.

Soak the All-Bran, sugar and dried fruits in the milk in a bowl for 30 minutes until the milk has been absorbed. Stir in the flour and turn into the loaf tin. Bake for about 1 hour.

Alternative suggestion
The mixture of dried fruits can be varied within the given quantity – chopped stoned dates, chopped figs and mixed candied peel – and up to 50 g/2 oz chopped nuts can be added.

Bran fruit loaf (*top left*), Fig loaf (*top right*, see p.123), Herb bread (*bottom*).

WALNUT BRAN BREAD

MAKES 2 × 450-g/1-lb LOAVES
Per loaf: 1,070 Cals, 61 g fat, 15 g fibre

75 g/3 oz 81% wheatmeal self-raising flour (see page 108)
75 g/3 oz 100% wholemeal flour
2.5 ml/½ tsp ground cinnamon
pinch salt
5 ml/1 tsp bicarbonate of soda
25 g/1 oz bran
100 g/4 oz walnuts, chopped
100 g/4 oz brown sugar
60 ml/4 tbsp vegetable oil
5 ml/1 tsp grated orange rind
1 egg
150 ml/5 fl oz low-fat plain yoghurt

Heat the oven to 190°C/375°F/Gas 5. Grease 2 × 450-g/1-lb loaf tins.

Sift together the flour, cinnamon, salt and soda and add any bran remaining in the sieve. Stir in the bran and the chopped nuts.

Beat together the sugar, oil, orange rind, egg and yoghurt. Beat into the dry ingredients. Pour into the loaf tins. Bake for 1 hour, or until a skewer pierced through the centre comes out clean. Stand the tins on a wire rack to cool a little before turning out.

BANANA AND RAISIN TEABREAD

MAKES 2 × 450-g/1-lb LOAVES
Per loaf:1,130 Cals, 38 g fat, 12 g fibre

150 g/5 oz 81% wheatmeal self-raising flour (see page 108)
75 g/3 oz 100% wholemeal flour
5 ml/1 tsp baking powder
pinch salt
5 ml/1 tsp ground cinnamon
150 g/5 oz brown sugar
3 bananas, mashed
75 g/3 oz margarine, melted
100 g/4 oz seedless raisins
2 eggs, lightly beaten

Heat the oven to 180°C/350°F/Gas 4. Grease 2 × 450-g/1-lb loaf tins.

Sift together the flours, baking powder, salt and cinnamon and add any bran remaining in the sieve. Stir in the sugar, add the bananas, margarine, raisins and eggs and beat for 3 minutes until smooth. Turn the mixture into the loaf tins and bake for 50 minutes to 1 hour, or until a skewer pierced through the centre comes out clean.

Stand the tins on a wire rack to cool slightly before turning out.

Serving suggestions
The teabread is much tastier if left to mellow for 2–3 days wrapped closely in foil. It can be served thinly sliced and spread with low-fat soft cheese or made into sandwiches with thinly sliced apples or mashed bananas.

FRUIT BUNS

MAKES 12 BUNS
Per bun: 190 Cals, 5 g fat, 4 g fibre

275 ml/½ pint warm milk
  and water, mixed (see page
  110)
65 g/2½ oz sugar
15 g/½ oz dried yeast
450 g/1 lb 100% wholemeal
  flour
5 ml/1 tsp salt
5 ml/1 tsp mixed spice
2.5 ml/½ tsp grated nutmeg
50 g/2 oz mixed candied peel,
  chopped
50 g/2 oz currants
50 g/2 oz margarine, melted
1 egg, beaten
warm milk and water to glaze

Pour the milk and water into a small bowl, stir in 5 ml/1 tsp sugar, sprinkle on the yeast and 100 g/4 oz of the flour. Stir and leave in a warm place for about 30 minutes.

Mix together the remaining flour, salt, spices, all but 5 ml/1 tsp of the sugar, the peel and currants. Mix the margarine and egg into the yeast mixture and pour on to the flour. Mix well until the dough leaves the sides of the bowl clean.

Turn on to a lightly floured surface and knead for about 10 minutes until smooth and elastic. Wrap loosely in greased polythene and leave in a warm place until doubled in size.

Turn out the dough and knead for 3–4 minutes.

Heat the oven to 190°C/375°F/Gas 5. Grease and warm a baking tray.

Divide into 12 pieces, shape into balls and place well apart on the baking tray. Cover loosely with greased polythene and leave in a warm place to double in size.

Bake for 15–20 minutes. Remove from the oven. Dissolve the remaining sugar in a little warm milk and water and brush over the buns.

SPICED ROCK CAKES

MAKES ABOUT 12 CAKES
Per cake: 165 Cals, 7 g fat, 2 g fibre

225 g/8 oz 81% wheatmeal
  self-raising flour (see page
  108)
pinch salt
5 ml/1 tsp mixed spice
100 g/4 oz margarine
75 ml/3 oz brown sugar
50 g/2 oz raisins
50 g/2 oz stoned dates, finely
  chopped
1 egg, lightly beaten
approx 15 ml/1 tbsp milk to
  mix

Heat the oven to 200°C/400°F/Gas 6. Lightly grease a baking tray.

Sift together the flour, salt and ginger and add any bran remaining in the sieve. Rub in the margarine until the mixture resembles fine breadcrumbs. Stir in the sugar, raisins and dates. Beat together the egg and milk, pour on to the dry ingredients and mix to a stiff dough, using a little more milk if necessary.

Place heaped teaspoonfuls of the mixture well apart on the baking tray. Bake near the top of the oven for 15 minutes, until well risen and firm.

127

RAISIN AND HAZELNUT BUNS

MAKES 12 BUNS
Per bun: 105 Cals, 5 g fat, 2 g fibre

100 g/4 oz 81% wheatmeal self-raising flour (see page 108)
2.5 ml/½ tsp salt
50 g/2 oz sugar
50 g/2 oz margarine
50 g/2 oz seedless raisins
50 g/2 oz All-Bran
50 g/2 oz hazelnuts, chopped
1 egg, beaten
approx 75 ml/5 tbsp milk

Heat the oven to 200°C/400°F/Gas 6. Grease 12 deep bun tins or paper baking cases.

Mix together the flour, salt and sugar. Rub in the margarine until the mixture resembles fine breadcrumbs. Add the raisins, All-Bran and hazelnuts. Beat in the egg and enough milk to make a soft dropping consistency. Spoon into the tins or cases on a baking tray and bake for 12–15 minutes, until well risen and springy. Leave to cool slightly before turning out. Serve warm, or very fresh.

MUFFINS

MAKES 18 MUFFINS
Per muffin: 122 Cals, 2 g fat, 2 g fibre

250 g/9 oz 100% wholemeal flour
175 g/6 oz strong white bread flour
5 ml/1 tsp baking powder
2.5 ml/½ tsp salt
100 g/4 oz brown sugar
5 ml/1 tsp bicarbonate of soda
415 ml/15 fl oz milk
25 g/1 oz margarine
30 ml/2 tbsp clear honey

Heat the oven to 220°C/425°F/Gas 7. Grease 18 deep patty tins.

Sift together the flours, baking powder and salt and add any bran remaining in the sieve. Stir in the sugar and make a well in the centre. Dissolve the soda in the milk. Gently melt the margarine and honey, pour on to the milk mixture and stir well. Pour on to the dry ingredients and stir to make a smooth batter. Pour into the tins and bake for 15–20 minutes, until springy to the touch. Allow to cool slightly in the tins before turning out.

Serving suggestion
Serve lightly toasted with thick dried fruit purée and low-fat soft cheese.

Raisin and hazelnut buns (*above*), **Muffins** (*below*).

128

POTATO BISCUITS

MAKES ABOUT 36 BISCUITS
Per biscuit: 40 Cals, 2 g fat, 0.5 g fibre

100 g/4 oz 100% wholemeal flour
5 ml/1 tsp salt
100 g/4 oz rolled oats
75 g/3 oz margarine
100 g/4 oz mashed potatoes

Heat oven to 170°C/325°F/Gas 3. Flour a baking tray.

Mix together the flour and salt and stir in the rolled oats. Rub in the margarine and knead in the mashed potato. Knead until firm and smooth.

Roll out on a lightly floured surface to about 3-mm/⅛-in thickness and cut into 7.5-cm/3-in rounds with a biscuit cutter. Place the rounds on the baking tray and bake for 15–20 minutes, until crisp but not brown. Transfer to a wire rack to cool.

Serving suggestion
These biscuits go well with cheese or soup, instead of bread.

DIGESTIVE BISCUITS

MAKES ABOUT 16 BISCUITS
Per biscuit: 115 Cals, 2 g fat, 2 g fibre

225 g/8 oz 100% wholemeal flour
225 g/8 oz medium oatmeal
50 g/2 oz brown sugar
50 g/2 oz margarine
50 g/2 oz golden syrup
a little milk

Heat the oven to 180°C/350°F/Gas 4. Grease a baking tray.

Mix together the flour, oatmeal and sugar and rub in the margarine. Melt the syrup in a small pan, cool slightly and pour on to the dry ingredients. Mix with just enough milk to give a firm dough. Turn on to a lightly floured surface and knead lightly until smooth. Roll out to 6-mm/¼-in thickness and cut into rounds with a 6-cm/2½-in biscuit cutter. Transfer to the baking tray and prick all over with a fork. Bake for 20 minutes. Allow to cool slightly, then transfer to a wire rack. When cold, store in an airtight tin.

See photograph on pp.132–3.

COCONUT BISCUITS

MAKES ABOUT 20 BISCUITS
Per biscuit: 110 Cals, 6 g fat,
2 g fibre

100 g/4 oz margarine
100 g/4 oz brown sugar
1 egg
225 g/8 oz 100% wholemeal
  flour
5 ml/1 tsp baking powder
grated rind 1 lemon
50 g/2 oz desiccated coconut

Heat the oven to 180°C/350°F/Gas 4. Grease a baking tray.

Beat together the margarine and sugar. Beat in the egg. Sift together the flour and baking powder, add any bran remaining in the sieve and stir in the lemon rind and coconut. Gradually stir the dry ingredients into the sugar mixture. Beat well and stir to make a firm dough. Turn on to a lightly floured surface and knead until smooth. Roll to 6-mm/¼-in thickness and cut into rounds with a 6-cm/2½-in biscuit cutter (or use a shaped cutter).

Transfer to the baking tray. Bake for 15 minutes, or until golden brown. Allow to cool slightly, then transfer to a wire rack to cool. Store in an airtight tin when completely cold.

See photograph on pp.132–3.

LAKELAND GINGER FINGERS

MAKES ABOUT 36 FINGERS
Per finger: 75 Cals, 4 g fat,
0.5 g fibre

175 ml/6 oz 100% wholemeal
  flour
2.5 ml/½ tsp bicarbonate of
  soda
5 ml/1 tsp cream of tartar
5 ml/1 tsp ground ginger
piece of grated nutmeg
50 g/2 oz rolled oats
175 g/6 oz margarine
100 g/4 oz brown sugar

Heat the oven to 170°C/325°F/Gas 3.

Sift together the flour, soda, cream of tartar and spices and add any bran remaining in the sieve. Stir in the oats and rub in the margarine. Stir in the sugar. Press the mixture into a greased 30 by 20-cm/12 by 8-in tin and level the top. Bake for 30 minutes. Cut into fingers and cool on a wire rack.

See photograph on pp.132–3.

OVERLEAF: Digestive biscuits
(*left*), **Coconut biscuits** (*centre*),
Lakeland ginger fingers (*right*).

7 FRUIT AND PUDDINGS

To be honest, this is a chapter that needn't be. For the healthiest way to end a meal is with fresh fruit, chilled and crisply fresh. But there are times when one likes to offer something hot, or to flatter guests with a dish that has taken care in the preparation.

First, fruit. Ring the changes by presenting different selections of fresh fruits in season, chosen for their appearance and texture as well as flavour.

Leave the skins on, if possible, both when eaten on their own or when used in fruit salads or other recipes.

Toss fruit in a tangy dressing of unsweetened fruit juice – apple, pineapple or orange with a dash of lemon juice – there is no need to mask the fresh flavour of the fruit by adding sugar; fruit contains its own natural sugar.

Avoid refined white sugar and opt instead for the moist brown sugars. A little goes a long way – and so it should for even unrefined sugar is calorie-packed.

If necessary, use dates, one of the sweetest fruits of all, to offset the tartness of fruits like cooking apples. Dried dates chopped into fruit pies and crumbles can take the place of sugar and add fibre.

Serve low-fat plain yoghurt or soft cheese (perhaps flavoured with spices) instead of cream, and use them instead of cream in recipes.

Use skimmed milk and polyunsaturated margarine whenever possible to minimize the fat and cholesterol content of puddings.

For a quick and easy dessert, mix fruit purée (made from fresh or dried fruits) with low-fat plain yoghurt or soft cheese. Chill, then top with toasted bran.

Thicken fruit juice and purée with wholemeal semolina for a low-calorie dish to serve with low-fat yoghurt or soft cheese. Use wholemeal semolina to thicken fruit in pies and flans, too.

Sprinkle toasted bran on to fruit desserts and add it to milky dishes.

Dried fruits are available all the year round for use in pies, tarts, sponges and crumbles and for simply stewing. A lightly spiced, hot dried-fruit compôte is an ideal winter pudding.

Lastly, don't feel guilty every time you don't make a pudding for the family. Rather, when you make one that is high in sugar and fats, you should feel guilty when you do!

RED FRUIT SALAD

SERVES 4
Per serving: 145 Cals, 6 g fat, 7 g fibre

275 ml/½ pint unsweetened apple juice
juice 1 lemon
30 ml/2 tbsp sweet vermouth
100 g/4 oz blackcurrants
100 g/4 oz raspberries, hulled
100 g/4 oz strawberries, hulled
100 g/4 oz black cherries, stoned
50 g/2 oz blanched almonds, toasted

Blend the apple juice, lemon juice and vermouth. Mix the fruits, pour the liquid over and chill for at least 1 hour. Just before serving, scatter with the nuts.

GREEN FRUIT SALAD

SERVES 4
Per serving: 110 Cals, 0 g fat, 3 g fibre

450 g/1 lb gooseberries, trimmed
8 green plums, halved and stoned
225 g/8 oz seedless green grapes
2 green apples, cored and thinly sliced
275 ml/½ pint unsweetened apple juice
30 ml/2 tbsp lemon juice
2 bay leaves

Mix together the fruits and bay leaves. Blend the apple juice and lemon juice and pour over the fruit. Chill well. Remove the bay leaves before serving.

FRESH FRUIT SALAD

SERVES 6
Per serving: 150 Cals, 3 g fat, 2 g fibre

150 ml/5 fl oz white wine
150 ml/5 fl oz orange juice
15 ml/1 tbsp lemon juice
225 g/8 oz seedless grapes
225 g/8 oz black grapes, seeded
2 oranges, segmented
2 apples, cored and sliced
2 bananas, sliced
25 g/1 oz shelled brazil nuts, halved

Mix the wine, orange and lemon juice. Put all the fruit into a bowl, pour on the liquid and chill for several hours. Stir in the nuts just before serving.

SERVES 4

Per serving: 460 Cals, 0 g fat, 7 g fibre

100 g/4 oz black grapes, seeded
100 g/4 oz seedless white
  grapes
4 apples, cored and thinly
  sliced
50 g/2 oz seedless raisins
15 ml/1 tbsp lemon juice
150 ml/5 fl oz unsweetened
  pineapple juice
150 ml/5 fl oz dry white wine

Mix the fruits. Blend together the lemon and pineapple juice and the wine. Pour over the fruit. Chill well.

BELOW: Banana and ginger cheesecake (*top,* see p.139), **Citrus fruit mousse** (*centre right,* see p.138), **Celebration fruit salad** (*bottom*). **OPPOSITE: Pineapple Romanoff** (see p.138).

CITRUS FRUIT MOUSSE

SERVES 4
Per serving: 150 Cals, 2 g fat, 4 g fibre

grated rind and juice 2 oranges
grated rind and juice 1 grape-fruit
15 ml/1 tbsp clear honey
10 ml/2 tsp powdered gelatine
150 ml/5 fl oz low-fat plain yoghurt
2 egg whites, stiffly beaten
90 ml/6 tbsp muesli base (see page 15)

Measure the juice and make up to 275 ml/½ pint with water. Put the rind, juice and honey into a small bowl, sprinkle on the gelatine, place over a pan of hot water until the honey has melted and the gelatine dissolved. Leave to cool.

Whisk in the yoghurt and leave until the mixture is on the point of setting. Fold in the beaten egg whites.

Spoon a little of the mousse into 4 individual serving glasses, sprinkle with the muesli and continue making layers, finishing with a topping of muesli. Leave in the refrigerator for 1 hour to set.

See photograph on p.136.

PINEAPPLE ROMANOFF

SERVES 4
Per serving: 175 Cals, negligible fat, 3 g fibre

1 medium-sized pineapple
grated rind and juice 1 lemon
grated rind and juice 1 orange
30 ml/2 tbsp brandy
225 g/8 oz raspberries or loganberries
2 bananas, sliced

Slice the top off the pineapple and carefully scoop out the flesh. Discard the top, the hard centre core and any discoloured spots. Cut the flesh into 2.5-cm/1-in cubes and put into a bowl with the lemon and orange rind and juice and the brandy. Cover and chill for at least 2 hours, or overnight.

Stir in the soft fruit and the banana. Pile into the reserved pineapple shell. Serve chilled.

See photograph on p.137.

BANANA FRUIT SPLITS

SERVES 4
Per serving: 145 Cals, negligible fat, 9 g fibre

100 g/4 oz redcurrants or strawberries
100 g/4 oz raspberries
30 ml/2 tbsp 100% wholemeal flour
4 large bananas
60 ml/4 tbsp low-fat plain yoghurt
25 g/1 oz walnuts, chopped

Gently heat the redcurrants or strawberries and raspberries in a small pan. When the juice runs, bring to the boil, sprinkle on the flour and stir until the fruit thickens. Boil, stirring, for 2 minutes. Remove from the heat and cool.

Peel the bananas, cut in halves lengthways and arrange in a dish. Pour over the fruit mixture, swirl with yoghurt and sprinkle with the walnuts.

FRECKLED MOUSSE

SERVES 4
Per serving: 190 Cals, 6 g fat,
2 g fibre

275 ml/½ pint milk
2 eggs, separated
50 g/2 oz brown sugar
few drops vanilla essence
100 g/4 oz wholemeal breadcrumbs
30 ml/2 tbsp orange juice
10 ml/2 tsp powdered gelatine

Heat the milk in a small pan. Whisk together the egg yolks and sugar and pour on the milk, beating. Return to the pan and stir over low heat until the custard thickens. Or cook in the top of a double boiler. Stir in the vanilla and leave the custard to cool. Stir in the breadcrumbs.

Pour the orange juice into a small bowl, sprinkle on the gelatine and heat over a pan of hot water until the gelatine has dissolved. Stir into the custard.

Whisk the egg whites until stiff and fold into the mixture when it is on the point of setting. Turn into a wetted 450-ml/1-pint mould and chill for 1½ hours. Unmould on to a serving dish.

Serving suggestion
Surround the mousse with a selection of fresh fruits – soft fruits such as raspberries, strawberries or black-berries; sliced peaches; apricots or bananas tossed in lemon juice; or halved plums.

BANANA AND GINGER CHEESECAKE

SERVES 8
Per serving: 250 Cals, 12 g
fat, 3 g fibre

Base:
225 g/8 oz digestive biscuits
  (see page 130), crushed
5 ml/1 tsp ground ginger
50 g/2 oz margarine, melted

Filling:
225 g/8 oz low-fat cottage
  cheese, sieved
150 ml/5 fl oz low-fat plain
  yoghurt
15 ml/1 tbsp clear honey
3 bananas, mashed
juice ½ lemon
10 ml/2 tsp powdered gelatine

Decoration:
2 pieces preserved ginger, sliced

To make the base, mix together the biscuit crumbs, ginger and margarine. Press into a greased flan ring on a greased baking tray. Leave to cool.

To make the filling, beat together the cottage cheese, yoghurt, honey, bananas and lemon juice. Dissolve the gelatine in 30 ml/2 tbsp water in a small basin over a pan of hot water, then stir into the banana mixture. Pour into the flan case and leave to set. Decorate with sliced ginger.

See photograph on p.136.

FROSTED ORANGES

SERVES 4

Per serving: 170 Cals, 4 g fat, 4 g fibre

4 large oranges
15 ml/1 tbsp orange liqueur
100 g/4 oz black grapes, halved and seeded
225 g/8 oz low-fat cottage cheese
60 ml/4 tbsp rolled oats, toasted

Cut a very thin slice from the base of each orange so that it stands firm. Cut the top one-third from each orange and carefully scoop out the fruit. Reserve the orange shells. Chop the flesh and put it into a bowl with the liqueur and grapes. Cover and chill overnight.

Put the cottage cheese into a bowl, stir in the toasted oats and the fruit mixture. Pile into the orange shells, making a high mound. Serve chilled.

ABOVE: Frosted oranges (*left*), Snowy mountain (*centre, see* p.142), Summer pudding (*right, see* p.142).

OPPOSITE: Rice figgy pudding (*top*, see p.144), Baked apple pudding (*centre*, see p.146), Farmhouse fruit pie (*bottom*, see p.145).

SUMMER PUDDING

SERVES 6

Per serving: 160 Cals, 1 g fat, 15 g fibre

about 10 slices wholemeal bread, crusts removed
700 g/1½ lb soft fruits –
  raspberries, strawberries, blackberries, redcurrants, blackcurrants
2 apples, cored and thinly sliced

Decoration:
a few black grapes

Well grease a 1-litre/2-pint bowl or pudding basin. Trim 6 slices of the bread to cover the base and sides of the bowl and arrange them so that they overlap slightly. Be sure to leave no gaps between the slices.

Hull the soft fruit, strip it from the stalks and put in a pan with the apple slices. Heat gently until the juices begin to run, then cook over low heat until the fruit is tender. Remove from the heat.

Strain off the juice and pour gradually over the bread lining the bowl. Put half the fruit into the bowl and cover with a slice of bread. Reserve a few fruits for decoration. Add the remaining fruit and any juice and trim the remaining bread slices to cover the top. Cover with a plate or saucer that fits inside the rim of the bowl. Stand a weight (such as a can of tomatoes) on top to press the plate firmly on to the pudding.

Leave in a cool place overnight. Run a knife round between the bread lining and the bowl, cover the bowl with a large serving plate, hold the two firmly together and turn upside-down, shaking slightly to release the pudding. Decorate around the base with the reserved fruits and black grapes. Slice to serve.

Serving suggestion
Chilled low-fat plain yoghurt beaten with a large pinch of cinnamon and the grated rind of 1 orange.

See photograph on p.140.

SNOWY MOUNTAIN

SERVES 4

Per serving: 150 Cals, 4 g fat, 1 g fibre

50 g/2 oz rolled oats
45 ml/3 tbsp whisky
15 ml/1 tbsp clear honey
juice 1 lemon
225 g/8 oz low-fat cottage cheese, sieved
150 ml/5 fl oz plain low-fat yoghurt, chilled
50 g/2 oz stoned dates, chopped

Spread the oats on to a baking tray and lightly toast under a grill or in the oven at low heat. Allow to cool.

Stir together the whisky, honey and lemon juice, then gradually beat into the cottage cheese and yoghurt. Stir in most of the toasted oats and the dates.

Divide between 4 tall serving glasses and sprinkle with the remaining oats. Serve chilled.

See photograph on p.140.

COCONUT ORANGES

SERVES 4
Per serving: 165 Cals, 6 g fat, 8 g fibre

6 oranges
15 ml/1 tbsp orange liqueur (optional)
2 apples, cored and thinly sliced
40 g/1½ oz desiccated coconut, toasted

Squeeze the juice and grate the rind of 1 orange and put in a bowl with the liqueur, if used. Peel and thinly slice the remaining oranges and remove any pips. Add the oranges to the bowl, cover and chill for 4–5 hours, or overnight.

Stir in the apples, transfer to a serving dish and sprinkle on the coconut. Serve at once.

DANISH BERRY PUDDING

SERVES 8
Per serving: 65 Cals, 3 g fat, 10 g fibre.

1 kg/2 lb 4 oz redcurrants, stripped from stalks
1 kg/2 lb 4 oz raspberries, hulled
60 ml/4 tbsp wholemeal semolina
sugar or honey to taste
30 ml/2 tbsp soured cream
30 ml/2 tbsp blanched flaked almonds, toasted

Put the fruit into a pan over low heat and stir until the juice begins to run. Simmer until it is tender. Purée in an electric blender, or push through a nylon sieve. Return to the rinsed pan, sprinkle on the semolina and slowly bring to the boil. Stir frequently over low heat until the grains are tender and the purée has thickened – about 20 minutes. Taste and stir in sugar or honey if necessary.

Allow to cool slightly, then turn into a glass serving bowl or individual dishes. When cool, spread the soured cream in a thin layer over the top. Chill. Just before serving, scatter with the almonds.

EDWARDIAN ICE CREAM

SERVES 6
Per serving: 195 Cals, 11 g fat, 4 g fibre

150 ml/5 fl oz whipping cream, chilled
275 ml/10 fl oz low-fat plain yoghurt, chilled
50 g/2 oz icing sugar, sifted
150 g/5 oz wholemeal bread-crumbs
30 ml/2 tbsp rum or Madeira
2 eggs, separated
225 g/8 oz raspberries, hulled

Whip the cream until just stiff, then whisk in yoghurt. Fold in the icing sugar and breadcrumbs. Beat together the rum or Madeira and the egg yolks and fold into the mixture. Whisk the egg whites until stiff and fold in. Turn into chilled freezing trays and put in the freezer or the freezing compartment of the refrigerator at its lowest setting. Freeze for 2 hours. To serve, transfer to the main compartment of the refrigerator for about 1 hour. Spoon into 6 serving glasses and top with the raspberries.

CARDINAL CREAMS

SERVES 4

Per serving: 270 Cals, 13 g fat, 6 g fibre

50 g/2 oz brown short-grain rice
25 g/1 oz brown sugar
2.5 ml/½ tsp ground cinnamon
575 ml/1 pint milk
15 g/½ oz powdered gelatine
5 ml/1 tsp vanilla essence
150 ml/5 fl oz low-fat plain yoghurt
50 g/2 oz flaked almonds, toasted
225 g/8 oz raspberries, hulled

Put the rice, sugar, cinnamon and milk into a pan, bring to the boil, partly cover the pan and simmer, stirring occasionally, for about 40 minutes, or until the rice is tender and the milk has been absorbed.

Put 45 ml/3 tbsp water into a cup or small bowl, sprinkle on the gelatine and heat in a pan of hot water to dissolve the gelatine. Stir 30 ml/2 tbsp of the gelatine mixture and the vanilla essence into the rice. Leave to cool, then beat in the yoghurt and most of the almonds. Spoon into 4 individual serving glasses.

Melt the remaining gelatine mixture and stir into the raspberries to glaze them. Spoon on top of the rice, decorate with the reserved almonds and chill.

APRICOT CREAMS

SERVES 4

Per serving: 235 Cals, 6 g fat, 18 g fibre

225 g/8 oz dried apricots, soaked
3 bananas, sliced
150 ml/5 fl oz low-fat plain yoghurt, chilled
30 ml/2 tbsp single cream
2.5 ml/½ tsp ground cinnamon

Garnish:
25 g/1 oz desiccated coconut, toasted

Purée the apricots, bananas, yoghurt, cream and cinnamon. Divide between 4 individual serving glasses and leave to chill. Sprinkle with the toasted coconut just before serving.

Alternative suggestion
Other dried fruits can be used in the same way – dried pears or peaches are particularly good. Add a pinch each of mixed spice and grated nutmeg.

RICE FIGGY PUDDING

SERVES 4

Per serving: 285 Cals, 8 g fat, 8 g fibre

40 g/1½ oz brown short-grain rice
575 ml/1 pint milk
25 g/1 oz brown sugar
2 eggs
175 g/6 oz dried figs, soaked and cooked

Put the rice and milk into a pan, bring to the boil, partly cover and, stirring occasionally, simmer for about 40 minutes or until the rice is tender and the milk has been absorbed. Stir in the sugar and allow to cool slightly. Beat in the eggs.

Heat the oven to 190°C/375°F/Gas 5. Grease a baking dish.

Arrange the figs in the base of the dish and pour on the rice mixture. Bake for 15 minutes, or until the top is brown. Serve hot.

See photograph on p.141.

BLACKCURRANT TAPIOCA

SERVES 4
Per serving: 95 Cals, 0 g fat, 11 g fibre

500 g/1 lb blackcurrants, stripped from stalks
150 ml/5 fl oz orange juice
40 g/1½ oz tapioca
40 g/1½ oz brown sugar
ground cinnamon

Garnish:
a little brown sugar

Put the fruit into a pan with the orange juice and cook until the fruit is just tender. Turn the fruit into a nylon sieve and drain off the juice. Pour the juice back into the pan, heat to just below boiling point and sprinkle on the tapioca. Stir well. Simmer, stirring occasionally, until the tapioca is soft.

Meanwhile, press the fruit through the sieve. Stir the fruit purée and the sugar into the tapioca, remove the pan from the heat and leave for 5 minutes to cool. Divide between 4 individual serving bowls. Sprinkle with a pinch of cinnamon and a few grains of sugar to decorate. Serve chilled.

WHOLEMEAL MACARONI PUDDING

SERVES 4
Per serving: 220 Cals, 7 g fat, 7 g fibre

50 g/2 oz wholemeal short-cut macaroni
575 ml/1 pint milk
25 g/1 oz brown sugar
1 egg, beaten
100 g/4 oz dried apricots, soaked and drained

Heat the oven to 180°C/350°F/Gas 4. Grease a baking dish.

Put the macaroni and milk into a pan, bring just to the boil and simmer for 10–15 minutes, or until tender. Remove from the heat, stir in the sugar and leave to cool slightly. Stir in the beaten egg.

Arrange the apricots in the base of the dish and pour on the macaroni. Bake for 30 minutes, or until the top is brown. Serve hot.

FARMHOUSE FRUIT PIE

SERVES 8
Per serving: 285 Cals, 14 g fat, 5 g fibre

Filling:
50 g/2 oz fine oatmeal
2.5 ml/½ tsp ground cinnamon
2.5 ml/½ tsp ground ginger
pinch ground cloves
grated rind and juice 1 lemon
500 g/1 lb cooking apples, cored and sliced

Pastry:
350 g/12 oz 100% wholemeal flour
5 ml/1 tsp salt
125 g/5 oz margarine
approx 60 ml/4 tbsp water
milk to glaze

Heat the oven to 200°C/400°F/Gas 6.

To make the filling, mix together the oatmeal, spices, and the grated lemon rind and juice. Toss the apples in the spice mixture.

To make the pastry, mix together the flour and salt and rub in the margarine until the mixture resembles fine breadcrumbs. Mix with just enough water to form a stiff dough. Turn on to a lightly floured surface and knead lightly until smooth. Divide in half.

Roll out one piece and line a 23-cm/9-in tart tin. Spread the fruit over the pastry and dampen the edges. Roll out the remaining dough, cover the pie and brush with milk. Trim and pinch the edges together to seal. Re-roll the trimmings, cut into decorative shapes, such as leaves, and place on the pie. Brush with milk.

Bake for 35–40 minutes. Serve hot or cold.

See photograph on p.141.

BAKED APPLE PUDDING

SERVES 4

Per serving: 330 Cals, 15 g fat, 9 g fibre

75 g/3 oz wholemeal bread-crumbs
30 ml/2 tbsp All-Bran
200 ml/7 fl oz milk, boiling
25 g/1 oz margarine
2 eggs, separated
50 g/2 oz sultanas
50 g/2 oz stoned dates, chopped
25 g/1 oz brown sugar
pinch ground cinnamon
450 g/1 lb cooking apples,
  cored and chopped
1 apple, cored and thinly sliced
5 ml/1 tsp melted margarine
25 g/1 oz walnuts, chopped

Put the breadcrumbs and All-Bran into a bowl, pour on the boiling milk, stir in the margarine, cover and leave for about 30 minutes until all the milk has been absorbed. Beat in the egg yolks one at a time, then the sultanas, dates, sugar and cinnamon; stir in the chopped cooking apples.

Heat the oven to 190°C/375°F/Gas 5. Grease a baking dish.

Whisk the egg whites until stiff, then fold into the apple mixture. Turn into the dish and bake for 35–40 minutes, until well risen and golden brown.

Arrange the sliced apple in a line down the centre, brush with the melted margarine and sprinkle with the chopped walnuts. Return to the oven for 4–5 minutes. Serve hot or cold.

See photograph on p.141.

BAKED APPLES

SERVES 4

Per serving: 210 Cals, 3 g fat, 16 g fibre

4 large cooking apples
8 large prunes, soaked and
  stoned
8 dried apricots, soaked and
  chopped
approx 15 ml/1 tbsp sultanas
15 g/½ oz margarine
150 ml/5 fl oz orange juice

Heat the oven to 190°C/375°F/Gas 5.

Core the apples, then fill the prunes with chopped apricots and pack 2 stuffed prunes into each apple – the cavity may have to be enlarged slightly. Press in the sultanas to fill in the gaps. Put a knob of margarine on each apple. Prick or slit the apple skins. ·

Stand the apples upright in a shallow baking dish which they just fit into and pour on the orange juice. Bake for about 40–45 minutes, until the apples are tender. Do not let them collapse. Serve hot.

Alternative suggestions
Any dried fruit, or mixture of fruits, can be used to fill the apples – currants, seedless raisins, sultanas, chopped figs. Chopped nuts give a good contrast in texture, particularly with 'floury' varities of apple. A little shredded coconut sprinkled over the fruit 10 minutes before the end of cooking time is good too.

APPLEOAK PUDDING

SERVES 6
Per serving: 425 Cals, 10 g fat, 4 g fibre

40 g/1½ oz margarine
100 g/4 oz rolled oats
25 g/1 oz brown sugar
50 g/2 oz 81% wheatmeal
self-raising flour (see page 108)
2 eggs
275 ml/½ pint milk
500 g/1 lb cooking apples, cored and sliced
2.5 ml/½ tsp ground cinnamon

Heat the oven to 190°C/375°F/Gas 5. Grease a 20-cm/8-in square baking tin.

Melt the margarine in a pan over low heat, stir in the oats and sugar and remove from the heat. Stir in the flour. Beat together the eggs and milk and gradually beat in to the oats mixture.

Arrange half of the apple slices on the base of the tin. Cover with the oats mixture, smoothing the top. Arrange the remaining apples on top and sprinkle with the cinnamon. Bake for 50–55 minutes, until the filling is set. Serve hot or cold.

APPLE BROWN BETTY

SERVES 6
Per serving: 300 Cals, 10 g fat, 14 g fibre

50 g/2 oz margarine
225 g/8 oz muesli base (see page 15)
grated rind and juice 1 orange
500 g/1 lb cooking apples, cored and sliced
225 g/8 oz dried apricots, soaked and drained

Heat the oven to 180°C/350°F/Gas 4.

Melt the margarine and stir in the cereal and orange rind. Pour the orange juice and 30 ml/2 tbsp water into a 1-litre/2-pint baking dish. Arrange a layer of apple slices and apricots. Spread over a layer of the cereal mixture and continue in layers, finishing with the cereal. Bake for 35–40 minutes, until the topping is golden brown. Serve hot.

APPLE AND DATE CHARLOTTE

SERVES 4
Per serving: 150 Cals, 6 g fat, 5 g fibre

90 ml/6 tbsp wholemeal breadcrumbs
500 g/1 lb cooking apples, cored and thinly sliced
50 g/2 oz stoned dates, sliced
15 ml/1 tbsp clear honey
15 ml/1 tbsp water
grated rind and juice 1 lemon
pinch ground cloves
25 g/1 oz margarine

Heat the oven to 180°C/350°F/Gas 4.

Grease a 575-ml/1-pint baking dish and dredge with breadcrumbs. Arrange a layer of apples in the dish and sprinkle with all the dates and some of the breadcrumbs. Continue making layers of apples and crumbs, finishing with breadcrumbs.

Gently heat the honey, water, lemon rind and juice, cloves and margarine in small pan until well blended, then pour over the pudding. Pat down well with the back of a spoon. Bake for 1¼–1½ hours, or until the top is crisp and golden brown. Serve hot.

APPLE CHEESE PANCAKES

MAKES 8 PANCAKES
Per pancake: 120 Cals, 7 g fat, 4 g fibre

100 g/4 oz 100% wholemeal
  flour
large pinch salt
1 egg
275 ml/½ pint milk

Filling:
225 g/8 oz low-fat soft cheese
75 g/3 oz stoned dates, chopped
2 apples, cored and chopped
grated rind and juice 1 lemon

To serve:
lemon wedges

Mix together the flour and salt and make a well in the centre. Break in the egg, pour on half of the milk and beat well. Beat until the batter is smooth, then stir in the remainder of the milk. Beat well and leave to stand for at least 30 minutes.

To make the filling, beat together the cheese, dates and apple. Stir in the lemon rind and juice.

To cook the pancakes, heat a heavy-based non-stick frying-pan, pour in a little of the batter and tip the pan to cover the base. Cook over high heat until the pancake bubbles. Toss over and cook the other side. Stack the pancakes and keep warm while cooking the remainder.

Divide the filling between the pancakes and roll them up. Serve on a heated serving dish with the lemon wedges.

Alternative suggestion
Other chopped, dried fruits can be used in place of the dates – raisins, currants, candied peel or apricots are good. And chopped banana can replace the apples.

ORANGE PUDDING

SERVES 8
Per serving: 540 Cals, 20 g fat, 11 g fibre

2 large oranges
175 g/6 oz stoned dates, finely
  chopped
2 cooking apples, cored and
  grated
2 large carrots, grated
150 g/5 oz wholemeal breadcrumbs
175 g/6 oz 100% wholemeal
  flour
5 ml/1 tsp mixed spice
pinch salt
175 g/6 oz seedless raisins
40 g/1½ oz brown sugar
100 g/4 oz margarine
2 eggs, beaten

Bring a large pan one-third filled with water to the boil. Grease a 1½-litre/3-pint pudding basin. Thinly pare the rind from 1 orange, cut it into thin strips and reserve. Grate rind from second orange and reserve. Remove pith and pips from both oranges and chop the flesh.

Mix together the orange flesh, dates, apples, carrots, breadcrumbs, flour, spice, salt, raisins, sugar, margarine and grated orange rind. Gradually beat in the eggs.

Sprinkle the base of the basin with the sliced orange rind. Spoon the mixture into the basin, cover with greased foil, tie securely and stand on a trivet in the pan. Put on the lid and steam for 3½ hours. Top up the water level as necessary with boiling water so that it comes half-way up the sides of the basin. Turn on to a heated serving dish.

GRILLED ORANGES

SERVES 4
Per serving: 60 Cals, 0 g fat,
3 g fibre

6 *large oranges*
10 *ml/2 tsp brown sugar*
1.5 *ml/¼ tsp ground cinnamon*

Cut the oranges in half, cut away the flesh from each section, and discard the tough membranes. Pile the contents of 3 orange halves into each of 4 half-orange shells. Mix together the cinnamon and sugar. Just before serving heat the grill and sprinkle the sugar over the 4 orange halves. Place under the grill until the sugar bubbles and the oranges are heated through. Serve at once.

BAKED PEACHES

SERVES 4
Per serving: 355 Cals, 15 g fat, 6 g fibre

8 *large peaches*
6 *digestive biscuits (see page 130), crushed*
75 *g/3 oz ground almonds*
grated rind and juice 1 orange
200 *ml/7 fl oz sweet white wine*
25 *g/1 oz brown sugar*

Heat the oven to 180°C/350°F/Gas 4.
Dip the peaches in boiling water for a few seconds, remove with a slotted spoon and skin them. Halve the peaches and remove the stones. Mix the biscuit crumbs with the almonds and orange rind and divide the mixture between the peaches, sandwiching the halves together again. Secure with wooden cocktail sticks. Place the peaches in a shallow baking dish which they just fit into, pour on the wine and orange juice and bake for 15 minutes, basting occasionally.
Heat the grill to high. Sprinkle the peaches with sugar to cover and grill for about 2 minutes, until the sugar caramelizes. Serve hot.

Alternative suggestions
Crushed ginger biscuits can be used instead of digestives. Orange or apple juice can replace the wine for the sauce.

COCONUT BANANAS

SERVES 4
Per serving: 315 Cals, 12 g fat, 4 g fibre

8 *small bananas*
30 *ml/2 tbsp clear honey, melted*
50 *g/2 oz desiccated coconut*
30 *ml/2 tbsp desiccated coconut, toasted*

Garnish:
1 *orange, quartered*

Heat the oven to 180°C/350°F/Gas 4. Grease a shallow baking dish.
Peel the bananas and brush them with the melted honey. Roll them in coconut and arrange them in the dish. Bake for 20–25 minutes, turning once, until the coconut is crisp. Sprinkle with toasted coconut and decorate with the orange wedges. Serve hot.

FRUMENTY

SERVES 4
Per serving: 260 Cals, 4 g fat,
6 g fibre

200 g/7 oz whole wheat
850 ml/1½ pints water
pinch salt
25 g/1 oz brown sugar
2.5 ml/½ tsp ground cinnamon
pinch ground ginger
75 g/3 oz currants

Garnish:
25 g/1 oz walnuts, chopped

Simmer the whole wheat with the water and salt in a large, covered pan for 1¼–1½ hours or until tender and all the water has been absorbed. Mix together the sugar, spices and currants, stir into the grain mixture and continue cooking for 5 minutes. Turn into a heated serving dish, sprinkle with the nuts and serve hot – or allow to cool, and serve with stewed fruit.

Serving suggestion
Serve it hot with stewed plums, apricots or spiced apples or pears.

HALF-PAY PUDDING

SERVES 6
Per serving: 195 Cals, 9 g fat,
3 g fibre

75 g/3 oz 81% wheatmeal
self-raising flour (see page
108)
5 ml/1 tsp baking powder
5 ml/1 tsp mixed spice
pinch grated nutmeg
75 g/3 oz wholemeal breadcrumbs
15 g/½ oz brown sugar
65 g/2½ oz margarine
a little milk to mix
100 g/4 oz mixed dried fruits
– currants, sultanas and
seedless raisins

Bring a large pan of water to the boil. Grease a pudding basin. Sift together the flour, baking powder and spices and add any bran remaining in the sieve. Stir in the breadcrumbs and sugar and rub in the margarine. Add just enough milk to mix to a soft dropping consistency. Stir in the dried fruits.

Turn into the bowl or basin, cover with greased foil, tie securely and stand on a trivet in the pan of boiling water. Cover the pan and steam for 2 hours, topping up the water as necessary with boiling water. Turn out the pudding on to a heated serving dish. Serve hot.

WEIGHTS AND MEASURES

Measurements are given in both metric and Imperial throughout. Use one system or the other, do not combine them. 1 lb has been rounded up to 500 g except in the baking chapter, where, to follow customary baking usage, it is given as 450 g.

The spoon measurements used throughout are always level. 1 teaspoon (tsp) = 5 ml; 1 tablespoon (tbsp) = 15 ml. To ensure success, check the size of spoons you are using.

Occasionally, bean and rice weights are given as cooked. The dry weight of beans is about half that of cooked; for rice, about one-third.

The energy value for each serving or portion is given in calories (Cals). If you are more at home with the new system of kilojoules (kJ), simply convert the calorie figures to kilojoules by multiplying by 4.2.

Unless otherwise stated, all the herbs are fresh. If using dried herbs, generally use one-third of the amount, although the freshness of the herbs will affect the flavour.

ACKNOWLEDGEMENTS

The publisher would like to thank the following organizations for their help and co-operation: For assistance with the photos: ALLINSON (cover and pages 25, 65, 80, 109, 113, 117, 124, 129, 132–3, 141); Buxted Poultry Ltd (cover and pages 93, 97); Green Giant Foods Ltd (canned Niblets sweetcorn pages 41, 85, 97); the Kellogg Company of Great Britain Ltd (cover and pages 16–17, 25, 37, 61, 85, 124, 141); Record Pasta Foods Ltd (cover and pages 37, 49, 61, 65, 93, 105); the Potato Marketing Board (pages 41, 76–7, 89); the Sea Fish Industry Authority (pages 41, 85, 88–9); and Whitworths Holdings Ltd (cover and pages 29, 48, 52, 69, 76–7, 93, 105, 109, 131, 141).

For providing props and other materials for the photographs: Eden Vale Ltd; Elizabeth David, Bourne Street, London, W1; Divertimenti Ltd, Marylebone Lane, London, W1; and Dickens & Jones Ltd, Regent Street, London, W1.

INDEX TO RECIPES

Page numbers in *italic* refer to the illustrations. Recipes marked with the * symbol are suitable for freezing.

E

Edwardian ice cream*, 143
eggs, scrambled with crispy
bran cakes, 24; 25

F

farmhouse fruit pie*, 145; 141
fennel and walnut salad, 51
fig: loaf*, 123; 124
  rice figgy pudding, 144; 141
fish: cobbler*, 91
  Creole*, 88; 88
  fish and corn chowder*, 40;
  41
  fish and sweetcorn
  casserole*, 87; 85
  fishcakes with onion sauce*,
  90
  kebabs with sweetcorn, 87;
  85
  Norfolk fish pie*, 89; 89
  ratatouille*, 91
  See also haddock
flageolet beans: cauliflower
  and bean salad, 50
fresh and dried beans, 72; 73
flans, savoury*, 81–3; 80
fresh fruit bowl, 13
fresh fruit muesli, 15; 16–17
fresh fruit salad, 135
fruit and nut bran, 13
fruit (dried): compôte*, 28
  foam, 20; 21
  fruity bran, 12
fruit buns*, 127
fruit flakes, 12; 16–17
fruit salads, 13, 53, 135–6; 136
frumenty, 150

G

gardener's pie*, 74
garlic: 'butter'*, 83
  chive and garlic dip*, 46; 44
ginger: banana and ginger
  cheesecake*, 139; 136
  Lakeland ginger fingers*,
  131; 132–3
gnocchi with tomato sauce*, 63
good morning scones*, 24; 25

grapefruit: and apricot salad, 18
  citrus cups, 14; 16–17
  marmalade, 18

H

haddock (smoked): baked
  Finnan potatoes, 86
  kedgeree, 86
  seafood salad, 57
  spiced fish soufflé, 90
half-pay pudding, 150
haricot beans: beans
  Provençale*, 72; 73
  two-bean and leek salad, 54
hazelnut and raisin buns*,
  128; 129
herb bread*, 125; 124
honey fruit loaf*, 122
hoppin' John*, 79
hummus*, 55

I

ice cream, Edwardian*, 143
Italian tuna tomatoes, 47

K

kedgeree, 86
kedgeree, lentil*, 68; 69
kibbled wheat loaf*, 118
kidney beans: beef and bean
  pot*, 104; 105
  cauliflower and bean salad*,
  50; 49
  chicken and bean paella*,
  94; 93
  melon and bean salad, 56
  red bean flan*, 82
  soup*, 39
  spiced beans*, 72
  two-bean and leek salad, 54

L

Lakeland ginger fingers*, 131;
  132–3
lamb: and artichokes*, 100
  guard of honour with
  walnut stuffing, 102

and pasta hot-pot*, 100
  pilaff*, 101
  stuffed cabbage leaves, 101;
  105
lasagne, vegetable*, 62
leeks: potato and leek soup*,
  40; 41
  soya bean and leek soup*, 35
  two-bean and leek salad, 54
lentils (brown): curry*, 70
  kedgeree*, 68; 69
  salad*, 54
lentils (red): cakes*, 71
  pie*, 71
  spiced lentil soup*, 38; 37

M

macaroni: and broccoli
  casserole*, 61; 60
  stove-pot*, 63
  tomato and pasta bake*, 64
  wholemeal macaroni
  pudding*, 145
malted milk, 19
marmalade, grapefruit, 18
melon and bean salad, 56
morning malter, 19
mousse: citrus fruit mousse*,
  138; 136
  freckled mousse*, 139
muesli: base, 15
  fresh fruit muesli, 15; 16–17
  toasted muesli, 15
muffins*, 128; 129
mushrooms: aubergine and
  mushroom flan*, 81; 80
  celeriac and mushroom
  salad, 51
  spaghetti with mushroom
  and walnut sauce, 66
  pasta and mushroom soup*,
  34
  stuffed mushrooms, 27

N

noodles, veal balls with, 104;
  105
Norfolk fish pie*, 89

Other titles in the series ✖

THE BACK – RELIEF FROM PAIN Dr Alan Stoddard
Patterns of back pain – how to deal with and avoid them

STRESS AND RELAXATION Jane Madders
Self-help ways to cope with stress and relieve nervous tension, ulcers, insomnia, migraine and high blood pressure

BEAT HEART DISEASE! Prof Risteard Mulcahy
A cardiologist explains how you can help your heart and enjoy a healthier life

OVERCOMING ARTHRITIS Dr Frank Dudley Hart
A guide to coping with stiff or aching joints

ASTHMA AND HAY FEVER Dr Allan Knight
How to relieve wheezing and sneezing

PSORIASIS Prof Ronald Marks
A guide to one of the commonest skin diseases

DIABETES Dr Jim Anderson
A practical new guide to healthy living

VARICOSE VEINS Prof Harold Ellis
How they are treated, and what you can do to help

HIGH BLOOD PRESSURE
Dr Eoin O'Brien and Prof Kevin O'Malley
What it means for you, and how to control it

MIGRAINE AND HEADACHES Dr Marcia Wilkinson
Understanding, avoiding and controlling the pain

DON'T FORGET FIBRE IN YOUR DIET Dr Denis Burkitt
To help avoid many of our commonest diseases

THE DIABETICS' DIET BOOK
Dr Jim Mann and the Oxford Dietetic Group
A new high-fibre eating programme

GET A BETTER NIGHT'S SLEEP
Prof Ian Oswald and Dr Kirstine Adam

ECZEMA AND DERMATITIS Prof Rona MacKie
How to cope with inflamed skin